I0140342

TRIBALIZE NOW:
THE PRACTICE OF BELONGING

James T. Barfoot

Stillpoint Publishing
Spokane, Washington

Cataloging Data
Barfoot, James T., 1955 -
Tribalize Now: The Practice of Belonging / by James T. Barfoot - 1st ed.

ISBN 978-0-9828747-2-1
Printed in the United States of America.

Stillpoint Publishing / Stillpoint Press
Eve Costello, Publisher
Spokane, WA U.S.A.
www.mystillpoint.net

Acknowledgments

This book is written with a great deal of gratitude for Bart Anderson, a man who had the most profound effect on my life. Bart was "Ten Bears," the embodiment of the Spiritual Teacher often written about in books on spiritual growth, and he drew his teachings from many disciplines. Ten Bears, the spiritual elder of the Wolf Clan, was a Shaman and a Zen Master, pulling up tools from any modality that was needed to deliver his message directly to the inner consciousness. He was a most loving and patient man and a constant taskmaster, encouraging me always to go deeper, in search of my truth. He instructed me to seek the function of all things and to understand that form is only the vessel. He had an extensive "bag of tricks" that he used to help all that he encountered touch that which is precious within themselves.

Words are always inadequate when attempting to describe this man who had such a profound effect on my life. He had a unique quality in his ability as a spiritual teacher to express his wisdom through everyday experience. One of the greatest lessons he left me was his zest for life. He never hurried, yet approached all tasks with a vision of completion in mind. His passing in July 2007 inspired me to dig deeper within myself and to more fully integrate the lessons learned over the previous twenty years. He had informed me many times that he was a teacher of teachers, and it is only recently after much soul searching that spirit has shown me that this is my true path. Within these pages is the medicine that I discovered on my own journey home. It was unfolded from within myself over the years I was mentored by Ten Bears, and continues to evolve.

A special note of gratitude is offered to my brothers and sisters of the Wolf Clan, who continue to practice and share the teachings. Some of the members of this group include: Michael Hoffman, whose recent book *Your Natural Gift* succeeds in delivering the essence of Bart's teachings and has provided me with numerous insights as I put the finishing touches on this work; Ann Coughlin, whose big heart and intuitive gifts are always offered unobtrusively at the right time to those in need; Steve Young, who has been there with me over the years, standing strong in his view of the medicine as we encourage each other to dig down deeply and find our true expression of it; Eve Costello, who is an outstanding Yoga instructor with a unique ability to put words to her feelings and express hers with gentle strength; my brother Bob Barfoot, who shares this journey by walking with joy in his heart and strength and clarity in his actions; and my wife Midge, who completes this circle with her willingness to share her beautiful heart without reservation. I am honored to be a member of this group and to witness the variety of sweet medicines that continue to grow from this common seed. As Ten Bears stated, "There are no orphans in the Wolf Clan, as all are invited to join with us."

Each of us is shaped by our experiences, and while Ten Bears and the Wolf Clan have been the dominant force in my transformation process I have many others to thank. The first would be Stuart Mauro, a Doctor of Chinese medicine whom I began studying with in 1986 in Dallas, TX. Stuart was my first Chi Kung teacher and it was through him that I discovered the power of movement and breath for centering and health. We formed the Dallas Chi Kung Association and sponsored numerous workshops. He also guided me to study Tai Chi and Pa Kua with Drs. Richard Peck and Iva Lim-Peck, also in the Dallas area. To this day I continue to practice and teach many of the forms that Stuart taught me. I am currently studying with Zhong (Steve) Wang in Spokane, WA, who is opening my eyes to another level of practice.

In 2008 I completed my accreditation in Clinical Hypnotherapy and NLP with Michael Bennett of Bennett/Stellar University in Seattle, WA. Michael is an artful practitioner who shares his knowledge and insights with enthusiasm. After working on my own that year, I was hired by a group that specializes in hypnosis in Spokane, WA. The nearly six years I spent with them gave me the opportunity to hone my skills while witnessing the inherent strengths and weaknesses to this type of change strategy.

In March 2013 I had the good fortune of attending a retreat with Stephen Gilligan, PhD, in Leavenworth, WA, where we were invited to experience his Generative Trance work. Stephen completed his Doctoral dissertation at Stanford while working with Milton Erickson, MD – the father of modern hypnotherapy – and his explanation of the evolution of hypnosis over this past century is helpful in understanding where we are headed with this book. Early 20th-century hypnosis treated both the conscious and subconscious mind as idiots that needed to be subdued and then programmed to achieve results. Ericksonian methods involved by-passing the conscious mind, which was viewed as an obstacle, through the use of indirect communication to the subconscious mind, which was viewed as remarkably intelligent. Generative Trance, in Stephen's words, invites the conscious mind to become a co-participant. This enables us to become truly creative, and mindfulness plays a big part in this. Stephen calls this the third generation of hypnosis and sees it as an opening to our Quantum field of possibilities.

My assertion is that the generative trance state he is referring to is the very state used by tribal people during ceremony and talking circles to engage the creative consciousness. This is a state that involves a dropping off or dissolution of identity that I have witnessed so many times in ceremony. This frees us from our fixed perspective and opens us to our Primal Nature, Buddha Nature or our Quantum field of possibilities.

Ruben Habito is another person that I wish to thank for pointing me towards these spaces within myself. He is the Zen Master of the Maria Kannon Zen Center in Dallas, TX – a Sangha where I sat regularly throughout the mid '90s to early 2000s. It is here that I experienced my first series of sesshins. The word sesshin literally means "touching the heart-mind" and involves a period of intensive meditation.

Towards the end of 2008, I was looking for a sesshin that was within a day's drive of Spokane, WA, and I was pleased to find the Great Vow Zen Monastery in Klatskanie, OR. This monastery is under the stewardship of Co-Abbots Jan Chozen Bays and Laren Hogen Bays, and it is here that I completed four annual 6- to 7-day retreats. I enjoyed the inviting atmosphere of the Sangha and the feeling of intention within this group that is generated after a few days of silent retreat.

Throughout many years of sitting and ceremony I was always focused on attaining something. Over the years I had many glimpses of this state that exists beyond ego attachment. Some were only moments, while others were more profound. What I discovered is that these are just remembrances of who we already are and that there is in fact nothing to attain.

I have learned that lasting change is a spiritual practice that involves a shift on the level of our Intentional Core. This Intentional Core is composed of our perceptions of the world. The ceremonies and shamanic journeying that we will engage in are experiential by nature and are designed to facilitate this shift. There is nothing formulaic about this process, and the tools I present are but markers on the road of life constantly inviting us to remember our way home.

Shelby Allison is a very talented young artist whose illustrations help capture the frustrations we feel when we are seemingly held hostage by our behaviors. Thank you to Scott Fitzgerald for designing the front and back cover as well as graphic layout of interior illustrations of *Tribalize Now*. Eve Costello (mystillpoint.net) and Stillpoint Publishing receive my thanks for editing this manuscript and producing this book with clarity and love. Eve has studied with Ten Bears for many years and her clear understanding of his work helped to deliver my interpretation of it.

Introduction

After taking more than five years to bring this to fruition, I realize that the book I began writing was started with the intention on my part of completing this work within myself before sharing it. This is the order in which all things must unfold as there is only value in sharing who you are, not who you imagine yourself to be. I have known since I was a young child that I had something precious inside of myself that I wanted to share, yet many times when I attempted to do so, it fell on deaf ears. It was no one's fault as they were doing the best that they could with the level of understanding that they were holding. This is confusing for many children who, it seems, are born of one tribe and raised by another. It took me a long time to grasp this truth and that is what this book is about. We are born of a tribe of light and even though we may have shielded ours in order to survive, it is once again time to let it shine. Contained within these pages is an invitation to do just that! Your willingness to open your heart and share your light is the reason you are here; everything else is a fabrication, a story that is being told by those who have forgotten who they are. Come join with us, we are your tribe and we are here to shine!

Table of Contents

1. Awaken Your Primal Nature

During the more than twenty years that I spent in the presence of my teacher "Ten Bears" Bart Anderson, to whom this book is dedicated, I learned the difference between the theory and practice of what it takes to be "one of the people." This refers to the state in which one's Primal or Tribal Nature, and its accompanying sense of being a part of something much greater than oneself, has become a foundational attribute. Without this sense of belonging, even our best intentions are governed and acted upon from a sense of self protection.

When I first met Bart I was an egotistical thirty-two-year-old with a strong desire to be someone special. I believed that in order to survive in this world I would somehow have to convince others to give me my fair share. I was isolated and alone after a series of failed business and personal relationships.

I won't tell you that my time with Bart suddenly changed me for the better, as my core beliefs were pretty nicely tied to an identity that pushed others away through the use of cleverness and sarcasm. My path home was an arduous one that tested my teacher's patience many times. The fact that I made it through is a tribute to his skill and to my own stubborn perseverance. Within these pages is the Primal Toolbox, the result of that journey and my work with individuals who were empowered to change their personal stories, behaviors, and beliefs. This is my medicine, and my hope is that you will find it to be of use to you, on your own way home.

We are all Tribal People

We live in a world in which less than 10,000 years ago the tribal model was it! Our ancestors were tribal, and many of us can trace our lineage to a much more recent tribe or clan. Given man's length of time on this planet, we would have to say that most of it was spent living within a tribal context. It is this knowledge that caused me to question what it is about this model of relating that could be utilized and applied today in our modern, high-paced world.

The Last of the Dreamers

What I am about to share with you is a dream that humanity has dreamed for countless generations. It is one of a people born into connection with creation, with nature and all of its abundance. This feeling of being a part of something larger than ourselves is our Primal Nature, an element inherent in the being, and its development is no longer encouraged or sustained in today's world. As you read these words the last of these wisdom keepers are being eradicated in various corners of the globe. My prayer is that this insanity that is driven by our lust for land and resources will cease, allowing the last of the indigenous tribes to continue their ways of life.

This book is a tribute to our progenitors, as well as a call to all who read it to look within and ignite the flame of their own Primal Nature, thus choosing a purposeful and connected life. Though these keepers of the "sacred medicine" are all but gone, the path of heart they follow and its teachings are available to all, with the courage to honor their truth.

Reawakening the Sacred Medicine

This is an appeal to my Native American brothers and sisters (those who share a common heart), to seek out the elders and medicine people within your communities and ask them if they would be willing to share their teachings, visions and wisdom both within and beyond your tribe. It is my sense that their medicine is needed more now than ever. It is my hope that the young people born into tribes today will seek out the timeless wisdom of their elders and begin to share this message of connection in new ways.

This strong and vital medicine carried by indigenous peoples was of necessity withdrawn and hidden from the forces of oppression. The indignities suffered by tribal cultures the world over at the hands of those who sought their lands and labor is well documented. The fact that many of those perpetrators, mostly of white European descent, were fleeing the tyranny of religious oppression and class structure in their own homelands serves to remind us that though we may aspire to higher ideals we are often guided to act from the base emotions of fear and greed.

Native American teachers began to share their medicine over the previous century and many seekers of the sixties and seventies had exposure to these practices. Those who approached with clear intention and openness received valuable insights that helped them better understand their relationship to the world around them. Many others just looked at the experience as another cool thing to add to their spiritual repertoire. What I am about to share with you, if approached with conscious intention and perseverance, will change your life. My hope is that you will find your own sacred medicine and become a valued member of your tribe. Who that tribe is, as well as how you locate and join with it, is a central theme of this book. We will begin to discover our tribe as we engage in the creation of our new story, one that no longer divides us along racial, ethnic or socioeconomic lines.

I wish now to offer a prayer, for a people nearly decimated by those who invaded the continent. My prayer is that you will continue to rekindle your vision of connection until it burns so brightly that it will be seen by all who seek to share a common heart. Let this beacon awaken within each of us the truth that we are all "one of the people." It is my hope that this time around, the indigenous peoples of "Turtle Island" (North America) may be a key in the transforming force, for a return to a more connected and vital way of life on this earth.

Your Purpose Is to Discover Your Tribe

Change comes to us all, and those of us who are willing to anchor ourselves solidly to our true nature will find that though the world continues to swirl around us, with practice we can still choose to live the rich, full lives that we desire and deserve. The simplest meaning of the term Tribalize Now would be the formation of people into groups or tribes, though I see it as much more. I see the words Tribalize Now more as a description of an action: the practice of belonging. This practice, once engaged, has the potential to change our perception of the world and to open doors to others as well. The operative word is choose, as any form of belonging must be by choice, and this act of choosing is rooted in the gift of one's service.

I choose the term gift, as this is in no way to be viewed as a form of barter or exchange. Rather, this choosing to participate is a sacred act whose reward is in the offering itself. Belonging is in our nature, and it is my intention to provide these time-tested practices in the form of a toolbox that will aid you in the discovering and sharing of your value.

The Primal Toolbox

The toolbox, its development, and its application are my gift to you, and it is with a sense of irony that I reveal it. The truth is, that each of us is given this fine set of tools as our birthright, and as children we open it up and explore it only briefly. It is soon set aside and forgotten by nearly everyone on this planet. Imagine for a moment a world in which children are taught a series of time-tested practices, with the knowledge that this training will culminate in rites of passage into adolescence and adulthood. The child comes to understand each stage and, with it, the requisite responsibilities that assure the transformation into a valued member of their family and community.

Compare this to our own culture where perpetual adolescence has become our developmental cul de sac. Through challenging ourselves to pick up the tools of self responsibility, we find others who are willing to join with us in creating a future that values our individual contribution to the whole. This book is written for anyone who knows that deep inside themselves there is a mystery and a purpose that is yet to be revealed.

Awakening Our Shaman's Perspective

The Primal Toolbox, when utilized with intention, will enable you to create the full, rich life that you desire and deserve. Know that these are ancient tools that were employed throughout millennial time to maintain the integrity of tribes and societies who understood and applied them. These implements have since been lost to those who view the world through the lens of a reality that is grounded in a scientific determinism based on the Newtonian model. The spiritual context of the world that our tribal ancestors lived in was much more akin to the Quantum Physics model that has been evolving over the past one-hundred years. The motto "seeing is believing," once deemed to be a statement of fact, is today being replaced with the more intellectually challenging "believing is seeing." It appears that the veil of the material world was pierced first by the tribal shaman and then later by the physicist. We are pushing into a new frontier in which the world and the maps we are using to navigate it are constantly changing, yet the territory as well as the principles that govern our interaction with it remain the same. Our perception of reality and our reaction to it is regulated by the degree of conscious awareness that we bring to the present moment.

Surely There Must Be More?

This agreed-upon reality that almost all of us accept as the standard operating system of the human being is nothing more than a poorly negotiated treaty that leaves us dependent and at risk. This book is dedicated to reawakening that which is and always has been our truth. We are much more capable than we have been led to believe. When we begin to discover who and what we are, outside of the stories that we have accepted as our truth, we open ourselves to the possibility of creating something different.

What We Share Each Day Is Our Gift

The world for some is a dreary and difficult place to wake up to each morning, as joy itself becomes a concept twisted into having and getting. This quality that is intrinsic to the being now seems elusive. Joy acquired at others' expense is not joy! It is greed and avarice and our heart becomes weighted down by our inability to break this bond. This book is about practice, as theory is the territory of the learned!

I Am Nothing I Know Nothing: A Vision Quest

These are the words I spoke to Ten Bears as I stood before him. He pulled his knife from its sheath, placed it between my eyes and pulled downwards to my naval, then made a second stroke from left to right across my chest. "I return you to spirit, now enter the sequester," he replied, and gestured towards the enclosure. I crawled forward, touching my forehead to the ground with a prayer and disappeared into the darkness.

My first in a series of vision quests was now underway! It is only through our willingness to face our fears, to call them out into the light of clarity that we may rediscover how to walk the path of the human being.

The most precious commodity we have is also the most squandered. Once spent it can never be recouped, and though some are given more, the amount is secondary to its usage. I am of course referring to the time allotted to us. Each of us is given this life as a gift, though few of us view it as such! This very moment is all that is real for us; everything else is a past or future illusion. The challenge most of us face is that of trying to walk into our future without having fully integrated the lessons of our past. Fortunately, they will return again and again until the lesson is finally resolved. Beware, as the trickster or coyote has many lessons for us and seldom arrives in the same form. Ten Bears often used "coyote medicine" to teach us to be mindful of the choices that we make. We are born with free will, and with that said there are no dues-free decisions.

2. Community

Community is a word that is used so often that it has effectively become a generic term used to describe groups of people doing just about anything or living just about anywhere except in a real community. If you want to know what a real community looks like, hop on a plane and go find an indigenous tribe – and you better hurry because there are not too many left.

Just about every other reference you hear to community pertains to either a community of location or a community of interest. Saying that you live in the community of Eastridge or Westridge is just where you live – that does not make it a community. The other is a community of interest, and though you may find that you have more in common with this group than with your neighbors, it's still not a real community and will disappear when your interest wanes.

The Essence of Community

Though real communities are rare, the knowledge of what composes them is not entirely lost. The tools for developing sustainable community are alive and well in our collective unconscious and provide a rich road map of archetypal symbols and practices that guide us inexorably back to what I feel is the normal state of the being.

The essence of community is the foundation upon which it is built, and like any good support structure it must be composed of elements that will stand the test of time.

These tools and ceremonies that I am about to share with you form an enduring representation of human interaction that I call the "practice of belonging." It is based on the original form of community, "the tribe," and within it are contained the foundational elements required to form sustainable and lasting communities. This construct in its pure form nurtures and supports the individual's unfoldment of "primal nature." This "primal nature" is the undefiled state that is inherent in the being; each of us is born with it, though it soon becomes obscured. Over time, who we are and what we stand for can grow as dim as our reflection in an unpolished mirror.

The Dusty Mirror Conundrum

The dusty mirror presents us with an appropriate metaphor for the unconscious state of humanity in which we live. We are currently speeding recklessly into a future guided only by this very vague reflection of reality. We turn to all manner of experts to help us understand what is seen in the mirror and we soon become even more confused.

Our confusion stems from the fact that these experts are only able to focus on a tiny area of this mirror, polishing and interpreting and then defending their own small portion. Institutions both secular and religious are then built around these assumptions and credentials are offered to those who pass the test, ensuring that their view becomes the orthodox one.

This book is about standing outside of the secure walls of orthodoxy and inviting others to do so as well. There was a time in our not-so-distant past that we lived without walls that encircled us. We had no need of doctrine to tell us how to behave or interact with each other, as we were led by something much stronger. We were guided to discover and maintain our own clear reflection in the mirror by those whose charge it was to mentor us in this practice from a very young age. These wisdom-keepers ensured that the knowledge of this path of self discovery was kept intact for future generations.

The First Rule Is to Serve

I used the term "the practice of belonging" in the title as I feel that these words evoke a congruent message on both a conscious and a subconscious level. When we break down the meaning, it refers to the original form of social awareness that human beings are born with, the feeling of being a part of something greater than this individual body. It also refers to the practices that ensure this awareness is carried into adulthood, thus maintaining the integrity of the tribe. The tribal construct has survived intact for tens of thousands of years through the utilization and application of these practices, and can be found even today in some remote areas of the globe. Meanwhile, American democracy – the gift of our founders – is a mere 238 years old and may fall, not in the wake of civil unrest, but by experiencing a slow and lingering death at the hands of those who no longer understand the first rule of civilization: "With great power comes great responsibility," or the more aptly put, "To rule is to serve."

How May I Be of Service?

It is the understanding of the nature of service that I view as an entryway into this tried-and-true model of community. Grounded in this daily practice, members will truly begin to discover what it is to be a human being. Though the actualization of this process may vary in form, if the intent is pure the result will be more than satisfactory. We have within each of us a subconscious drive to be a part of something larger than ourselves and also to be a valued contributor within this circle of humanity.

Giving Is the Key to Receiving

It is with this in mind that I titled the first chapter "Awaken Your Primal Nature" as a term rooted in both the practices and the subconscious understanding of what it takes to create community. It is through the willingness to share our gifts that we actually open ourselves to receiving that which is offered. An open palm holds far more sand than a closed fist!

These actions run contrary to most of what we have been taught, and yet they are the most fundamental elements of healthy human interaction. Without the understanding and practice of "giving without thought of receiving," the circle is in effect broken.

This book is written with the intent of reaching individuals with a message of possibility and of envisioning our relationships in a new light. The structure upon which real community is built still exists, and we will explore how this form may serve us as we hold this vision firmly in our minds and walk boldly into the future we create.

Constant Through Time

The art of community formation has been around since mankind first grouped together around the fire utilizing natural formations such as caves for the protection and security of the clan. We evolved from clans and tribes to villagers, townspeople and city dwellers and yet the fundamentals remain the same. On a deep level we are seeking the same things that our ancestors did when they gathered together in their versions of community. Without certain essential elements, all we are capable of forming are loose associations around particular interests, which soon dissolve as they are based on temporary events.

When viewing these communities, the differences in them may at first appear to be indistinct. Don't people in tribal communities share the same interests and isn't that what keeps them together? Yes, they may appear to be very much the same until we dig deeper, and that is what we will begin to investigate. Let us begin by exploring what constitutes a tribal community and what it is that we can learn from this structure about building sustainable modern communities.

3. What Makes A Tribe A Tribe?

Typically a tribe or clan is composed of an extended family or families that live together. Their location may be fixed or they may move through a geographic area that shifts according to conditions such as weather, food source, security or political influences. All members of the tribe have a vested interest in staying together and derive benefits such as pooled labor, knowledge and security by doing so. Let's look more closely at this, as it seems that they may be a community of both interest and location. What does that mean and how is a tribal community different from some communities more familiar to us?

There are some definite traits in common between tribes and other communities, though there are some pretty distinct differences. We see that interest and proximity play key roles in all tribes, as without either of these elements a tribe would cease to exist. Compare that to modern communities and we may observe one or the other, though not usually both. Earlier we looked at neighborhoods and discovered that most were a community of location comprising people with divergent interests. Is there something more to tribal communities that we might discover as we seek to strengthen the bonds of modern communities?

Beyond Interest and Location

There are quantifiable traits and practices that exist within tribes and other groups that when identified give us the framework on which to build modern sustainable communities. The formulation of this approach is modeled on the principles and practices that have been successfully utilized by tribes since before recorded time. Through embracing this methodology, communities today have the capacity to evolve from groups of people with divergent aims located in the same geographic area to being a cohesive, asset-rich group united through a shared vision, story of accomplishment and common purpose.

Does this sound like the kind of community that you would like to live in? Now hold that thought in your mind as you continue to read this unfolding story of how ancient archetypes and practices may provide the time-tested keys to revitalizing modern communities.

From Dissonance to Resonance

The model that I am about to share with you is designed to move us forward as individuals, families and as communities. It is no surprise that what we term as a stuck community, one in which the focus is on fault and blame, is composed of individuals who quickly tune in to this same frequency. It is with utmost care and consideration that any dialogue to initiate change must begin. It is often those who appear to be most resistant in the initial phase that will become strong supporters of it, as they choose to become engaged in the process. This can only occur if we choose inclusive, forward-moving dialogue without marginalizing those who are in pain and may feel oppressed in a stuck community.

4. The Circle As Archetype

Our world is full of symbols that evoke feelings within us, and the one that may be the most primal of all is the circle. This represents in the larger view the collective sense of humanity and the world, though in its smaller form it is the gathering of the tribe around the fire at night. In an even "smaller" form it is the circle of the individual, the wholeness of a single being. It is this group around the fire that we will look at more closely for how we might utilize a deeper understanding of this nightly exchange as we begin the process of community building. What can we learn about this group that we can model in our version of the tribe? Why does the circle figure so prominently in our message of community?

Our ancestors created the very foundations of community around this fire! It provided warmth and security from predators and enabled the cooking of meals, though that was only the starting point. The really profound activity was the celebration that occurred within the circle through storytelling and enactment, which effectively transferred the wisdom and knowledge of the tribe to its membership. It is here within the fold of the extended family that a unique bond was formed.

Being "One of the People"

The message delivered around the fire was about much more than the development of new skills. It also contained the message of what the group stood for as "a people" and how each member's uniqueness completed the circle. This was not a group of isolated individuals drawn together out of fear or desperation, but a cohesive whole composed of members who viewed themselves as "one of the people" before acknowledging their own names.

This sense of belonging can only occur through a long process of acceptance born of deep caring for the others in the group. Is it possible to restore this sense of community within our small towns, our cities, or even through our social media connections?

Begin with Questioning the Status Quo

I believe that it is not only possible but also inevitable that we will once again find and restore value in the places that we choose to live and socialize. What we are witnessing now is the result of the slow-yet-steady dissolution of community around the globe. If we are to survive as a species, it will be through the restoration of meaningfully interconnected local communities. That can only be accomplished if we start to ask the hard questions. I intend for this to be a hopeful book that offers the promise of a new beginning – born of the realization that what we are doing now, collectively, is just not working.

5. The American Dream Hits the Wall

In the midst of economic upheaval on a global level, we are faced with social and political unrest as the middle class in the former industrialized nations continues to erode. The dream of a comfortable retirement evaporated in 2008 along with the nest eggs comprising once-bulging 401K and IRA accounts. The recovery of 2010 fueled by unprecedented money creation could so greatly diminish the value of the American dollar that it may soon lose its status as the world's reserve currency.

With stagnant wages and skyrocketing healthcare premiums over these past thirty years, many individuals were lulled into relying on increasing home values that they borrowed against to see them through. They now feel even more hopeless as they have become debt serfs tied to properties with negative equity. The Boomer generation represents a huge demographic that will not enjoy the same retirement that their parents did. Social security, the supposed safety net, is also predicted to be gone or dramatically altered in the near future. All of this leaves those who felt they had a secure retirement ahead looking more and more like they will have to continue to work for the foreseeable future. That is, of course, if they can find work.

Forget Global Warming and Just Come to Your Senses

If you were walking along a street in London or Paris in the fifteenth century, you would be watchful of bedpans being dumped from second-story windows. Anyone who hears of this practice today would be horrified by it. If we were to look back, from one or two hundred years into our future, would we not have the same disbelief regarding our current handling of pollution? People of the fifteenth century already had an understanding of the correlation between waste and disease, and rulers began imposing regulations on disposal of waste since as early as the fourteenth century, after suffering the Black Plague. The people had knowledge, they just did not act on it right away. Witness the recent oil-spill fiasco in the Gulf, as well as its associated finger-pointing and denial of responsibility amongst the offending parties. They claimed they were doing their best and that it was just an unfortunate accident, while they lobbied to remove more of the regulations that govern their behavior.

I believe that the problems associated with ongoing climate change and environmental pollution pose serious challenges that will only be met through the development of sustainable local communities. Before anything can change, whether personally or culturally, we must begin by accepting the reality of the situation and take action on a personal and then community level. The answer lies in being willing to address the potential consequences of our actions through the development and the use of Intentional Outcomes in our decision-making process.

This is a foundational tool within the Primal Toolbox that ensures that actions stem from Conscious Intention. The long-term benefits of this practice far exceed the short-term gratification associated with a linear, purely goal-oriented decision process based on false metrics. While the bottom line may be met while drilling deeper wells offshore in inaccessible areas or by using enhanced recovery techniques like fracking, what are the long-term consequences? We have been lulled into thinking that nothing else matters but the corporation and its shareholders. The rapid depletion of our resources serves to enhance their value, but to what end? Who benefits when the last of a species vanishes? We have been operating from an adolescent model that does not factor these elements into our equation.

We have become a society devoid of deductive reasoning, as it is no longer valued or taught in school or even in many colleges. We have become unthinking dispensers of facts that we have memorized just long enough to get a passing grade. Degrees issued from our bloated institutions now leave the graduates a possibility of a job, with a certainty of years of debt. The irony of this situation is that the educational system contains within itself all of the solutions to this very problem. There is plenty of talent and more than enough money to solve it, we just have to ask the questions that will encourage more productive outcomes. In order to do this we must step outside of the status quo and begin to create something new. Our children's futures are being squandered through our unwillingness to challenge our factory-based educational system.

Superficial Communication May Be a Distraction

Most of us spend our lives rushing from home to work and back in the midst of thousands of others like ourselves, and end our days feeling incredibly dissatisfied with it all. We want something more, and in that quest we have developed a very elaborate system of electronic communication to keep us informed and connected to numerous social networks both local and global. My question is: despite the wired nature of our lives are we perhaps more isolated than we realize? If you doubt the premise of this question, try turning off everything for a couple of days and then see how you feel without all the input.

You may discover that you are not alone in your sense of isolation, as most anyone who allows the distractions that we call modern life to subside will discover that they also have the same sensibility. We are so incredibly busy and also so incredibly alone that it begs the question, What is it that each of us is seeking, because there surely must be more? The always-on social networking scene as it stands today is merely the ego's attempt to give us the illusion of connection without risking anything. Is there value in this evolving process of interaction? Absolutely, though it will be most effective when used in conjunction with old-fashioned face-to-face communication.

Shopping for Love

Let's use online dating as an example that I can share with you, although my personal experience is not entirely current as I have been married for a number of years. Today, we are able to scan hundreds of potential mates or dates and perhaps connect with some online and begin discussions. These discussions may go on for days, weeks or perhaps months, with some individuals seemingly connecting deeply without having met in person. What happens when the couple finally meets? Has the online communication built a bond that will stand the test of a face-to-face meeting? Or will one or both be disappointed?

My thought is that nothing can trump that first few minutes of connecting in person! You will feel a spark or you won't regardless of all your previous online bonding. As sensory beings we are capable of engaging all of our senses only when we meet in person. So please use online dating as a door opener if it's right for you, but save yourself the long, drawn-out discourse (unless of course that is what you are seeking) and meet each other for coffee in a suitable place. I met my wife at an outdoor event and it was love at first sight. As luck would have it she felt the same way! Engaging with others in person may feel risky at first, though with practice it will open the doorway to the freedom of expression we desire.

6. Finding and Sharing Your Value

There is something within each of us that is aching to be discovered! Our desire to expose this precious feeling is so strong that in the past we likely did so in an environment that was non-supportive or even destructive. This resulted in our burying or even denying this beauty that is at the source of our being. This book is written with an intention of awakening this preciousness that is our Primal Nature.

It starts with the question of who we are and what we stand for, as individuals, as families and as communities. We begin the process by first laying down our desire to blame or point fingers, and then engaging in a practice that embraces a brighter future, one that is inclusive and is not dependent on outside forces to move us forward. The reason for this is directly related to acceptance of the part that we play in maintaining the status quo and our finding the determination to change it. Nothing lasting can occur unless the desired outcome is initiated and maintained from within the individual or the community itself.

Change is usually arrived at through the gates of hope or desperation, with the latter being the most utilized entryway. Most of us will tolerate a situation until it becomes unbearable before choosing to risk change. This fear of change binds us to the very object that we wish to be rid of, as we weigh the known feeling of oppression against the potential devastation that awaits us in the unknown. It takes Duty, Devotion and Purpose to push past this complacency born of fear, to open to new ideas and engage in the process of creating the desired change. The process of transformation that I am about to share with you is not new; it is in reality as old as humanity itself.

Tools for Life

The practices that form the foundation of a connected, fulfilling life are inherent in the being, and what I have done is frame them in a way that makes them accessible to all who choose to utilize them. I will share with you a Change Strategy that I refer to as the Primal Toolbox, which provides the framework and principles that foster the Relational Excellence through which both individuals and communities will thrive.

Creating Lasting Change

Primal Coaching utilizes the Primal Toolbox and directs development from the inside out. It will only be effective over the long term if the process is enacted in this manner. Change that is imposed from or dependent upon outside intervention, no matter how well intentioned, will cause only a temporary progression, at best, that may ultimately cause more harm than good. This does not preclude the offering of resources from outside to either a community or an individual; it is more about giving or receiving in line with the requirements of the situation. It is important to always consider the possible consequences when offering assistance or accepting it from others. Giving and receiving gifts without strings attached is seldom practiced in our culture, so please be careful what you ask for, as it may come with an agenda.

Giving According to One's Capacity

The practice of giving is a task that bears further discussion. We truly have few examples of this in our culture today. Christmas as it originated had some of these elements, wherein meals were shared and simple gifts (often handmade) were exchanged amongst family and friends. This practice has largely lost its original meaning, having long since become a retail-driven celebration of excess, with citizens encouraged to play their part by spending money they can ill afford to spend. Fortunately, at least for merchants, credit is provided to consumers who may add to their already heavy debt burden.

Be aware enough to give that which you can truly afford rather than risk bankruptcy or ruin to fulfill what you perceive to be expected of you. If we are honest with ourselves about what we are capable of giving and do so with intention, we may find that others also are pleased to rethink this process as well. The gathering together of friends and family and sharing of food and conversation is far more important than the obligatory gift exchange.

A Culture of Giving

An excellent example of gift giving with intention is the Potlatch Ceremony. The following is summary of a much more detailed explanation offered in Wikipedia:

A Potlatch is a gift-giving festival and primary economic system practiced by indigenous peoples of the Pacific Northwest Coast of Canada and the United States. The word in Chinook Jargon literally means to "gift" or "to give away," and the ceremony has played a key role in the redistribution and reciprocity of wealth.

At Potlatch gatherings, a family or hereditary leader hosts guests in their family's house and holds a feast for their guests, whom they honor through the giving of gifts. The status of an individual or clan is determined not by how much they possess but by how much they give away. This may seem an odd ritual when viewed through a Western cultural wealth model, where gifts are seldom given without consideration of benefits (whether publicity, prestige or tax). However, I believe wealth that is hoarded is of little service, while wealth shared is a measure of true abundance.

7. The Open Circle

This brings us to the observation that on the cover, the circle depicted is a "Zen Circle" and that the bottom is open. I believe it best conveys the attributes of a dynamic, evolving individual and community. Many tribes were able to flourish for hundreds – even thousands – of years through embracing this practice of openness. They willingly invited others into their circle in order to discover who they were, though this may seem unusual or perhaps judged to be naive when viewed through our modern eyes. We tend to be most comfortable with a closed circle and invite in only those who meet our criteria for approval.

Openness Leads to Fearlessness

Is this open circle a valid practice in today's environment? Or would one be inviting disaster by not being wary of strangers? In truth, community itself cannot form without a willingness to invite others in, and as individuals we must learn to embrace others whom we may choose to view as different from ourselves. This process of inclusiveness has the potential to create a rich diversity within communities and will provide each of us with the opportunity to challenge our old stereotypes.

We have in effect become a culture of individuals, and though we often celebrate independence as an ideal it seems somewhat misguided. The individuals that we elevate to celebrity status are often those who are least equipped to provide us with societal role models.

The Rebel Has Value – Invite It In

True independence is not born of opposition, but of acceptance. Or to put it in another perspective, how can we achieve independence without first allowing ourselves to truly belong? I believe that interdependence is the foundation upon which independence is built.

The traits that the rebel possesses are not so different from those of the hero. One walks inside the wheel of life while the other feels disconnected from it. Rebels in my view have a huge potential to be active contributors once they begin to feel valued by other members of their tribe. Understand the metaphor in this and discover what your own internal rebel has been saying to you. What is it really seeking after all?

Tribes Are the Primal Construct

It is for this reason that I have chosen tribal structures to model, as I view them as the most poignant examples of what community represents. As modern humans we have effectively removed ourselves from the "circle of life" and become isolated individuals constantly looking outward to define who and what we are. This leaves us constantly at risk, with so little in the way of genuine connection and affection that it is no surprise that most of us feel alone.

We are no longer taught to look inward for answers and consequently have chosen religion over faith as it is much easier to quote scripture than to take the responsibility demanded by faith. If we do so, then we must scrutinize ourselves before passing judgment on others. If we seek to create communities that exude the attributes of a just society we must first discover equanimity within ourselves. Development unfolds with careful and constant self examination, followed by implementation of practices within a group of individuals who are also determined to offer their own unique gifts by way of service to community.

Personal Growth Is a Tribal (Community) Concern

This is not an easy task for any group and yet the rewards to both the community and the individual are potentially enormous. I have taken a somewhat different approach from other books that focus on community building, in that I am presenting an examination of the individual in relation to the group as well as the journey toward being active and engaged citizens. The call to return to our Primal Nature is a message that provides the requisite spark from which the fire of community can be kindled. This is not to be confused with the belief that encouraging consciousness in individuals will automatically translate into a more cohesive community. This has already been tried within both the corporate and community-building worlds with little long-term success. What has been lacking is the framework within which consciousness and commitment are honored and directed towards the good of the whole.

Each individual must be celebrated and encouraged for the uniqueness that they bring to the table. Community thrives when those who are invited to guide the process do so with this in mind. Slowly the awakening of a common purpose begins to take place as individuals begin to participate in the creation of a group goal that is supported by an Intentional Outcome.

The process enacted in this manner is effective, in that it appeals to our Primal or "essential nature," and the implementation of a community-building model based on this has the potential to change our understanding of ourselves as well as the neighborhoods in which we choose to live. People become enthusiastic when they are valued, and soon begin to present gifts to the group that surprise even themselves.

It is this foundational mechanism that is often missing in our modern culture. We may grow up being told what to do and how to do it rather than being encouraged and rewarded for our service to the family and community. Children are sometimes viewed as being in the way when adults are busy doing tasks, and prime teaching moments are squandered. More to the point, the opportunity to allow that child to feel good about contributing is lost.

The barn raising was one such example of community activity that we look back on with nostalgia. While some may find it quaint, it strikes a chord with us, as it contains within it the elements of a healthy, vibrant community. What happened between then and now? At what point did we cease being citizens who took pleasure in contributing to shared tasks and simply became consumers who purchased our experiences? Today we are valued less for our heart or creativity itself and more by our productivity and what we can consume with it.

8. Tribal Role Models

The structures of tribes separated by vast distances – even continents – are surprisingly similar. It is my view that this is an occurrence that bears close examination as we seek to understand and apply these properties in relation to our current situation. That which has enabled indigenous people to sustain themselves over millennial time will surely have value when framed into the context of modern community restoration.

A Different View of Priorities

The discussion of tribal role models cannot begin without first examining our need as modern humans to impose an intellectual framework based on productivity and time management over what is essentially an eternal model devoid of these concepts. How is it that entire populations were able to thrive without embracing these measures of value?

This was accomplished through a deep trust that all would be provided as needed, not from some external force that could be manipulated to do so. It came from a knowing that we and nature are one.

Perhaps the question to ask is how have we survived as long as we have by living without regard for this inherent relationship? We are truly at a crossroads, and it is my hope that we will find it within ourselves to return to these age-old values and continue our journey back to the foundation of humanity. It is our disconnection from nature that has served to place us as a species on the very brink of annihilation.

Please note that the following roles I will be describing are generalized across a broad range of tribes and that there will always be exceptions in localized geographic regions. I am seeking to express the unique interactions that take place in the form of relationships between the particular roles within the tribe and regard these as archetypes of transformation. These are mantles that represent both the energy and intention that is expressed within a particular role. These roles are no longer interpreted as being gender based, but rather as integral parts of a unified whole, each fulfilling an equally important task.

When utilized by modern individuals, it is this view that will enable us to create an intention to step into and embrace these aspects as we discover our own tribe and our relationship within it. These are tried-and-true models that give us a look at the essential elements of community and the relationships around which it is formed.

Two Styles of Leadership

Every tribe has a chief whom we would view as the tribe's leader in the same way that we might describe modern CEOs, military commanders, or heads of state. This would be an erroneous assumption in that it is based on a different value system. We live in a culture that values individuals as units of production or consumption, and many of us will find with self examination that we either revere or despise those entrusted to lead us. This measuring is a sideways attempt by the Ego to find and express our value. It is a symptom whose origins lie in our inability to see ourselves as an integral part of the "circle of life" that all tribal cultures embraced.

This is precisely the difference between a modern leader and a tribal chief: one organizes the world he controls strategically as pieces on a chess board to maximize his return, be it profit or prestige, and the other makes decisions based on the good of the whole. It is important to understand that we play a part through our own abnegation of personal responsibility in the first case. We have instead chosen authority, and though we tout ourselves as a democracy, our lack of personal accountability is reflected in our choice of leaders. "We the people" has become "What's in it for me," and it is no surprise that we put in place leaders who are not averse to feathering their nests at the public expense. We must choose to join with others and create communities that are empowered to change from within, which requires both structure and dialogue that are nurturing and supportive without being overly idealistic.

It's an Honor and a Privilege to Lead Others

Let us examine the role that the chief fulfilled in the context of a tribe. The power of the chief does not lie in his ability to apply and enforce laws. Tribal cultures are not bound by laws in the same sense that we are bound by laws. If there are none to enforce, then where does the chief's ability to exercise his will come from? How is it that he is able to maintain order amongst hundreds or even thousands of members? There are some things stronger than laws: there are mores and values that are grounded in customs or virtues that provide a code that is implicit within the tribe.

The chief wields influence through who he is, and his strength is demonstrated by his actions. The chief lives as an example that his people can emulate, thus fulfilling the role of a true leader. Decisions that affect the wellbeing of the tribe are arrived at with lengthy discussions that afford individuals the opportunity to have their say. These discussions may be further reflected upon by a council of elders who in the tradition of many Plains tribes would "smoke on it."

The life of each chief and the stories of their bravery and accomplishments is woven into the rich fabric of the tribe and retold around the fire at night, instilling the spark of possibility in those who listen. The power of a chief is that of convener, one who facilitates the assembly and asks the important questions of his people. The first skill of any good leader is in the ability to create the structure within which community will thrive and then to step aside and let it take shape.

The Shaman Creates the Intention

The shaman is an essential member of all tribal structures, and though the name is derived from a Turkic-Mongol word it has become synonymous with a tribe's spiritual leader. In this book we will be exploring this role from the perspective of the function of relationship builder rather than the esoteric attributes and healing skills that the individual may possess. The primary function of the shaman is to unite the members of the group through the orchestration of ceremonial practices. These rituals are passed on from generation to generation by the shaman to those deemed worthy of receiving them. The shaman's role is to create the dynamic (sacred space) that ensures that the participants are afforded every opportunity to engage in practices free from preconceptions. Each member offers their intention under the instruction of the shaman, as a vessel that is open to receive the guidance and strength to fulfill their role as active tribal members. This offering of themselves is in effect their gift to the sacred circle, of which they are an intrinsic part.

The Keepers of the Wisdom

The role of the elders is to carry the wisdom of the tribe, demonstrate it by way of example, and share it through story telling. Though this practice has been largely lost in our culture, its reintroduction as a component of the Primal Toolbox has the potential to assist both stuck individuals and communities in releasing the old tale and creating a new one of possibility. This group used to be an intrinsic component within our own culture before our shift to media-driven consumerism and infotainment.

We still have within our society a rich resource in the form of those with profound wisdom born of experience, and it is imperative that we invite them to share this for the good of our communities. We have allowed the dissemination of information to usurp the knowledge of those who have painstakingly discovered their truth.

Change may be the only constant in life, but adopting and then discarding information and practices without fully integrating the requisite lessons may leave us in an ever-more-precarious state.

It is timely to once again observe the shift in communication as more individuals begin to utilize the developing social media networks to connect with one another. It will be interesting to witness the effect of this new medium on our world. It could be the beginning of the end for autocratically controlled media megaliths, though only if we abandon their message of scarcity and blame and assume the mantle of personal responsibility.

Mentoring Is an Act of Love

Within each tribe are societies that are charged with refining and spreading the traditions and skills that have kept the tribe intact for generations. It is important to note that women are warriors in some tribes around the world, though in most cases they form societies that hold the social fabric of the tribe together. They quite literally supply the skills that keep them fed and clothed and sheltered. These skills are passed on to their children with the understanding of the value of the service that it entails. It is the form the teaching takes within tribes that is so profound. Passing on one's skills to younger tribal members is a sacred act. The very survival of the tribe depends on it, and the teaching of those tasks is done in a serious-yet-joyful manner. The whole tribe celebrates the success of these new contributors. These apprentices understand that no member's task is more important than another, as each has their part to play in maintaining the wellbeing of the tribe.

Contrast this to our culture, where the first thing we ask each other upon meeting is, "So what do you do?" Our answer will serve to clarify our status in relation to the questioner, thus keeping everyone safe and in their box. The Toolbox is designed to get each of us out of our own boxes and back into life.

Your Life Is Your Ultimate Gift

The soldier societies are composed of warriors whose function is the protection of the tribe. It is easy to see these men simply as warriors, as that was their dominant role over the many generations in which they defended their people and homelands against the relentless expansion of empire and industry on all continents. The true function of these societies is much more akin to a protector provider and, as is the case with the woman's societies, these societies help create the glue that holds the tribe together. They provide the highest level of service and sacrifice, which many of the young men choose to aspire to. They are good hunters who pass on these skills to those who seek to join their ranks, though their greatest gift is the wisdom, ethics and character that they demonstrate through how they live their lives.

Membership in one of these societies is considered to be a great honor and these groups often competed with each other in skills demonstrations, hunting and in battle with hostile forces. In referring to "your life is your ultimate gift," the obvious meaning would be the giving of one's life to protect family or tribe. That is true, though the more important meaning to me is not how you die, but how you live. How each of us conducts ourselves each day has a huge effect on those in our circle.

Your Tribe Is Not Complete without You

The last group of tribal members as a whole is best viewed as an organism that is composed of individuals that enable it to function as a cohesive unit. Each person within the group is as a cell within the organism or tribe. Choosing to view ourselves from this place leaves no room for the petty manifestations of ego that are often associated with group dynamics. Each cell functions for the good of the whole that would not be complete without it. Cells develop unique characteristics and functions, as do individual members of the tribe, in order to ensure that the organism thrives. The thought that one function is more important than another is laughable when viewed from this context.

Standing Outside and Looking In

My comprehension of this comes from having spent most of my early adulthood standing outside of the "wheel of life" looking in at those who seemed to have a unique ability to bond with others. This way of conducting oneself was foreign to me and appeared to be very risky and ill advised. It always felt as if these people were giving up so much just to belong to this group. My interpretation was that these individuals had relinquished their freedom and that they were leaving themselves unnecessarily exposed. I now recognize that what they were giving up was their need to be special and separate. What each of us gives up when we choose to walk inside the "sacred or primal circle" is at best an illusion of independence that for most is a cover for defensiveness, fear and judgment.

Separation Is an Illusion

Earlier I stated that true independence is cultivated through interdependence, which is the foundation of all tribal communities. It is this understanding that when given enough weight will provide the opening through which each of us must step, if we are to become active members of community.

Some may be asking, Are we not, as human beings, all born inside this "primal circle" of creation, and if so, how do we seemingly let it slip away? The answer is that we are and that we simply forget who we are as individuals and as a people, and spend our lives trying to find a home that we truly could never leave in the first place. If this sounds a little like the plot of some bizarre comedic tragedy, then we must laugh together in acceptance before we can begin to see something more.

I have framed these role models in the current tense out of respect for the tribal communities that are remote enough to still continue the old ways. Very few people today have had the good fortune of being born into an intact tribal community. What I am referring to is a community that still practices the traditions that have sustained them in the past. To be born inside a community such as this is to be born inside the "wheel of life," with the thought of separation being as foreign to them as the thought of truly belonging is to most of us. These members are connected not only to each other but to everything around them. Nature is not something to be conquered and exploited but something to be celebrated as an extension of themselves. She never fails to provide that which is required to sustain them and for that they are grateful.

9. Practices that Foster Belonging

Tribal communities that have lasted for many hundreds, if not thousands, of years have done so only through keeping intact practices that celebrate the uniqueness of each member in terms of their contribution to the community. "How can this be?" we may ask. It sounds as if the individual is somehow being duped into relinquishing his or her identity to the group.

I do not ask that you agree with me, only that you allow yourself to question any resistance that you may feel as I have done for many years before arriving at this view point. I recall my initial sense of unease as I tried to grasp the meaning of this way of life. I was mentored by a man who constantly invited me to stand inside the "wheel of life," and it was rare when I did not leave some part of me on the outside still looking in.

Bring Your Body, Your Mind Will Follow

In other words, I was physically involved yet unwilling to surrender to the depth of the experience. Some part of me was holding back. That makes it easy for me to be empathetic to all who question the possibility of what I am proposing. I can also assure you nothing ever worth having is easy, and that there is a price of admission should you choose this path. I cannot promise you anything other than the value that occurs through the willingness to become an active participant in your own journey of discovery. What will that be? You must find that out for yourself. As I have been informed so many times, "Sometimes you just need to show up!"

The Source Code for Community

What I am offering is a tried-and-true model for the restoration of community! I have selected the core practices that tribes have used to foster a sense of belonging, a sense of connection with each member, so that we may experience and understand their value. It is crucial to look at these traditional practices before we look at the Primal Toolbox that has been formulated and adapted to fit our modern lifestyles. In either case, it is the intention that one creates and acts from that will determine the outcome, rather than the elaboration of form.

Whose Story Is It, Anyway?

The most significant thing that any of us can bring to this process is an acceptance of what is, and a belief in the possibility that we can create something beyond the story that we have been repeating ad nauseam in our minds. It is this story that each of us believes is so uniquely ours that really prevents us from experiencing the rich, full lives that we desire and deserve.

This story in all of its convoluted details and assumptions is acted out mostly in an unconscious state, ensuring that we remain at the effect of the external world. The feeling can be likened to a piece of wood swirling in an eddy outside of the stream of life. The amazing thing is that we spend a huge amount of time and energy trying to either defend or disprove this tale that we have been repeating. It is through the embracing and acceptance of this yarn that we can begin the process of self awareness that will guide us back to the stream of life. In the next chapters we will begin to open the Toolbox and explore these time-tested practices.

Holding Fast to the Facade Takes Energy

Our acceptance of the reality of the situation is arrived at through our willingness to investigate, embrace and then detach from circumstances that we have become so identified with. It is through this stripping away of these layers that we can continue the journey towards being active, engaged members of our community (tribe).

I Just Don't Seem to Fit In!

Once this facade begins to fall away, the energy that was used to maintain it will suddenly be available for creative pursuits, and this will be the commencement of a rebirth into possibility. Please understand that this is not a linear process, though it may at first appear to be so – it is a cycle, as is everything under creation!

We Were Trained to Be Square!

Man's greatest challenge is to simply acknowledge this and let go instead of resisting it. You and I were trained from birth to be something that we are not. We are apparently all square pegs in a round world, or at least it would appear so. Though this may seem to be a funny analogy, it seems appropriate when viewed from the feeling sense. Who hasn't felt cornered and oppressed, or that they just don't seem to fit in?

We Are All Shaped By Our Journey

This is our personal journey, and the understandings that we arrive at, that in effect round out who we are, enable us to fit into our community as valued members. Each of us is already on this journey of self discovery, and if you are reading this and have gotten this far, then something must be resonating with you. It is from here that we choose the practices that will challenge us to go deeper, and pull up the tools we need as we begin to walk inside the sacred circle.

10. Our Life Outside of the Wheel

This circle is an archetype that evokes a familiar feeling in us, a remembrance of being inside of the wheel of life. We have all had the experience of being inside of this primal circle from time to time throughout our lives. This process is one of returning to that which we find is our natural state of being. It is also a practice that with patience will afford us the deep sense of what it is that we have been depriving ourselves of all these years. It is this yearning that will in effect give us the fortitude and perseverance to continue the process.

Compassion and Understanding for our Behaviors

The part of us that is invested in our life as we are currently living it may be somewhat resistant to something as beautiful as life inside of the wheel. It is also important to recognize that all behaviors begin with a positive intention! How can that be, you might ask, when the results that I get after engaging in them are not productive? Behaviors are nothing more than unconscious patterns that we run each day; some are useful and many are not. Most often these unconscious patterns are attempts to recreate or avoid experiences or emotional states. We are in effect held captive by a belief system that prevents us from actualizing our desires. We spend our lives in a state of unresolved yearning for substantive connection with others and instead settle for superficial, controlled, and limited experiences we perceive as less risky. Our behaviors, and the outcomes that they generate, then reinforce this cycle of unconsciousness.

How does one engage in the process of becoming more consciously aware, you ask? The way out of this loop is through conscious awareness supported by action! Ok, that sounds good; but how do I get there? There are practices that you may engage in that will take you through progressive stages of awareness. The journey through these stages was taught instinctively in tribal cultures and we shall soon begin this progression ourselves. Without the learning and application of the tools of awareness, we are destined to lead a life at the effect of our world as we perceive it.

Awakening from the Long Sleep

This process of awakening is a staged process, one that is gradual and ongoing. Real change is incremental and must be supported by action that will sustain it! We live in a culture that celebrates overnight success as an ideal, when that is in fact a misdirect based on the premise that money and success are equivocal. Nothing could be further from the truth. The acquisition of wealth, power, or even spiritual insight by individuals who have yet to discover their own self-worth is sure to bring ruin. Before a person can be truly wealthy, they must first discover the abundance that is their birthright.

Whether you are the CEO of a major corporation or the Abbot of a monastery (insert your religious preference), you are faced with an equally difficult challenge. If you see your function as more than a role that you have chosen to play, then you may be attached to it or identifying through it. You may become very accomplished and highly regarded for what you do! You may even live out your life in the knowledge that you are a good person, but unless you are willing to step beyond the security of identity you will always be wanting. It is this wanting that has driven us on our path to excess! We have fallen far from the understanding of what it means to be "one of the people" abandoning our "tribal nature" for the trinkets of materialism.

We as individuals are not so different from the tribal people of the past, who gave up what they stood for when faced with what appeared to be overwhelming evidence that their perception of reality, as well as the beliefs and practices that sustained it, were no longer valid. While most tribes gave theirs up at gunpoint, our perceptions merely slipped away, one day at a time, until they were forgotten. We acquiesced as children when faced with a construct that did not support our innocence. We will all do what is necessary to survive!

This story is one of returning to a way of life that invites others to join with us in offering our gifts. The life that I am talking of is one that is lived within the sacred circle. It is rich, full, and abundant, and it is available to any who are willing to face themselves without pretense. It is never too late to find your value and to begin sharing it with others.

11. Entering the Sacred Circle

Choosing to enter the circle of life is a sacred act! That is a strong statement and I am being very deliberate with my words so as to be fully understood. If you are reading this book chances are that you are interested in joining or may already be active in a community-minded group, or perhaps you are seeking to enhance all your relationships. Either way, this stage must be handled with utmost care in order to rekindle the flame of your "primal nature."

In tribal communities across the globe, the understanding of this is acted out on a physical level, whereby members are invited to literally walk inside the "wheel of life" or "medicine wheel." Though the form varies from tribe to tribe, the intention remains remarkably the same. The act is that of surrender!

Surrender Is Far from Defeat

The circle is entered on one's knees while bowing to touch the forehead to the ground in an act of humility. The gateway faces east to greet the rising sun, which symbolizes newness, possibility, and innocence. Those who enter choose to do so with the understanding that they must leave all that they are, and all that they imagine themselves to be, outside of the "sacred circle." They enter as open vessels ready to receive guidance and to discover where they are in the "wheel of life." This process involves participants entering and journeying in a clockwise direction around the center until they each find their "spot." Standing or sitting in place they pray and wait with certainty that a message will be delivered to each of them. The communication they receive further strengthens their bond within the tribe. The wisdom gleaned from the experience, and then shared, does not elevate the individual as it is a gift that is given from the members to the group.

You Can't Get There from Here!

We must consider several things as we view this practice from our modern perspective. The first is that what is occurring is communication with the unconscious mind, and this is a much more direct process for tribal members raised in an environment that encourages and supports this process. The second is that our culture favors logic and reason and tends to group these practices in with the occult, or simply labels them as kooky fantasy. It is this type of bias that must be challenged within each of us if we are going to surmount the barriers of intellect and open ourselves to a broader and deeper experience of connection with our fellow man.

The Doorway to Freedom and Expression

This is not an entirely foreign experience. As young children we were much more open and receptive; we just stopped trusting this part of our nature. Most of us will remember that as children our summer vacations seemed to last forever and that each of us now perceives time as having sped up as we have grown older. Is this a normal function of what we deem to view as advanced or civilized culture? Or is it in fact a dysfunction? Is it even possible to live in a modern, high-tech world without being slaves to time and productivity? I would not have proposed the idea unless I believed in the possibility of creating a life without these restrictions.

It's Always Been There Guiding and Directing You

This book is a call to reconnect with our Primal Nature, that part of you that seeks to share and express your richness with family, friends, and community. This rekindling of an abundant inner life frees up our creative energy and gives us purpose and direction. In time we will learn to receive and honor the guidance that is available to each of us as responsible, self-aware individuals who recognize the value of belonging.

Unwrapping Your Gifts

I have selected the core practices that will give us an understanding of these ceremonies with respect to intention and implementation. These have been incorporated into a teaching that I call the Primal Toolbox, which applies practices that encourage each of us to become creative, engaged members of our community (tribe). This is the process of change that occurs from within self and community and can have a potentially profound effect on our country and our world.

12. Our Primal Nature

The term Primal Nature resonates with a message beyond the spoken word. It evokes an archetypal image that beckons us to return to something solid, grounded, and familiar. This is in no way an invitation to abandon our way of living in this modern world and return to a primitive lifestyle as lived by our ancestors. It is instead a call to peel back the layers of the mask that each of us wears, and in doing so reveal our own Primal Nature.

It is through the rediscovery of this aspect of ourselves that we may seek solutions to assist us on our path towards a life lived inside the wheel. What is this Primal Nature that I refer to? It is nothing less than an awareness of connection to everyone and everything. It is this sense that we were born with before the individuation process took hold and we began our culturally guided journey into an unfulfilled life.

Let me clarify that the process of individuation itself is a necessary and healthy part of the growth cycle. The challenge today is to attempt to foster growth and development in a society that in my view has skewed its priorities. We have come to believe that who we are is achieved primarily through acquisition of money and resources. Consequently we direct a disproportionate share of available time as individuals and as a nation toward this pursuit of wealth and power. This is nothing more than a misdirected and superficial expression of our internal drive for connection and abundance. The innocence and trust that we are born with soon become offerings to the gods of fear and insecurity.

Breaking the Cycle of Fear

Our greatest resource is our children, and yet even the best intentioned among us can only pass on to them our own understanding of the world and how we choose to view it. Despite all the wonderful talk about how spiritual today's children are, the reality is that without a strong set of values developed and shared within a group, the little ones may soon grow into isolated and lonely adults. It is up to us as adults to demonstrate what we stand for and to set in place a practice that invites our offspring to do the same.

It is with this in mind that I wrote this work and have tailored much of it toward providing adults with the tools and practices that will enable them to raise creative, vibrant members of society. In doing so we restore the cycle that has been broken and begin the necessary process of societal regeneration.

How Is that Working for You?

This brings us to the next step in our process of self discovery. This is where the renewal starts, with the awakening of possibility within each of us. Initially we begin with the act of surrender, by giving up our need to cling to our old way of life and the identity that it reinforces.

We in effect create space in our consciousness for the process of transformation to take place. This can be accomplished through a series of practices that I will lay out in more detail as we continue.

Haven't I been Here Before?

"The Practice of Belonging" is best viewed as a series of circles within circles, as this is anything but a linear process. This is something that is confusing to those of us who come from a logical and methodical approach to learning. No real inner work ever gets done through careful analysis that is devoid of emotion, as intellectual understanding can only carry us to the gate of consciousness and never through it.

The Circle Is a Spiral

As we are constantly in motion, our view of our world is always shifting. Much as with a spiral when looking from above, we appear to find ourselves in the same place after the completion of a revolution; when viewed from the side it becomes obvious that our perspective has shifted. The key is to allow this process of change to unfold naturally. Our frustration comes from seeking sameness in the midst of change. When we cease to cling to or attempt to control everything, we begin to discover the unique quality of each moment and our relationship to it. The challenge is to first be aware of and then question our resistance.

Your Behaviors Are Not So Unique!

Many of us were raised with a belief that we are somehow defective, or perhaps really special or better than our peers! Either way we spend our lives trying to disprove what we know to be lies. Many of the behaviors that we develop along the way serve to keep us trapped in a repetitive cycle of shame, negative self-nurturing or blame. No one is free of this, and yet freedom is a choice that begins with this thought. What is it that is most important? Defending our personal reality that really isn't working for us anyway? Or being willing to acknowledge that we desire and deserve more?

The beauty of this form is that it presents every opportunity for us to abandon our filtered experience of our world and begin to see it as it is. With a continuation of this process we will slowly discover the possibility of living a life inside the sacred circle. We are doing nothing more than returning to that which is our birthright, and in doing so embracing the full measure of our humanity!

13. Finding Our Primal Nature

As we begin our journey into the discovery of our Primal Nature, joining with others in the accomplishment of shared tasks will provide the opportunity for us to become more conscious of our interactions with them. The idea of joining with others as we develop and practice our newfound understandings may be more than a little threatening. How may I accomplish this, you may ask, as so many of the challenges that I face now are unique to me? We may sense that it would be better to work out these lessons or questions on our own before interacting with others.

I agree that some things are best kept to ourselves or only shared in a safe, supporting environment. We will learn practices that will assist us in walking with this openness while ensuring that we are able to keep it intact. This approach cultivates discernment in place of judgment to establish and maintain all of our relationships within parameters that foster healthy interactions.

Clear Intention Is Required

I believe that this task is best approached with the intention of developing and then offering our own unique gifts to the larger community. There will be time for solitude as well as time to gather together, and it is this interplay that will serve to shape our individual understanding of kinship. All relationships must begin with the question, "What am I here for?" If the answer is to make a difference or to offer your as-yet-undiscovered gifts, then you are prepared for the next action. The initiation of the process of setting the foundation of relationship in place will enable us to create bonds that surpass our previous experience.

Treading the One Great Path

This book is written with a different approach than many others that I have utilized on my path to understanding self. These books in fact are divided into two categories: those concerned with community transformation, and those dedicated to self transformation. This one invites us to engage in a practice of journeying into the circle to find ourselves and to develop the skills that will lead us to become valued members of our community (tribe).

You Are More Powerful than You Imagine

We will begin with some practices that will guide us into the discovery of who we are. We start by taking time to reflect on our personal story and how it affects ourselves and those that we interact with each day. The work that we will engage in is twofold, as it involves the integration of both our internal and external experience of the world. Until we align these experiences, our world is unbalanced and full of anxiety, stress and suffering.

The key to unlocking this process is our personal story and the understanding of its effect on the life that we are creating. The riddle is solved through the creation of a new personal story that is then acted upon each day with Duty, Devotion and Purpose until we become it.

Acting out our new story with pure intention is acknowledged by all of creation, and this has nothing to do with force of will. It is best addressed with a spirit of acceptance that the result is a given and that all that is required is our offering of time and energy towards this cause.

Force of will can also get things done, though it is usually fueled by a more basal energy that is derived from our attachment to an outcome and often accompanied by pride or resentment, the pride or resentment being a by-product of our expectation of that result and how others may receive it. It is far from the act of celebration engendered by the offering of our gift towards the unfoldment of our intention.

Whom Does Our Dialogue Most Affect?

In our culture, where words are dispensed with little consideration of their effect on others, to begin to discover their true power gives one pause. Understand that a word is a thought given a resonance and that it is the compulsion to speak without reflection that so often does damage to those who are closest to us. This pales in comparison to the damage that we inflict upon ourselves by replaying the worn recordings of our personal story, thus ensuring that the drama we call our life is acted out accordingly.

Connecting with Your Intention

The first lessons are dedicated to discovering the effect that our personal story may have on us, our relationships with others and also to discover what level of intention that we use as we interact with our world. It is this increasing intentionality over time that supports the unfoldment of our new personal story.

These exercises comprise four modules that contain lessons and practices that when integrated will carry us once around the "wheel of life." Each circuit when completed will bring us back to the start with a fresh view of our world and our place in it. Each of these is a point of entry to the understanding of self, and we will begin our journey by crawling on all fours through the eastern gate.

Humility Is the Entryway into True Strength

The idea of crawling may seem unappealing and submissive, though it is actually the polar opposite. There is nothing weak about this action as it is requires great courage to engage in this process of humbling oneself. In doing so we begin allowing something new into our arena and allowing the transformational process to unfold. The eastern gate is the gate of possibility, and to enter this gate we begin by preparing an offering in the form of our old story. This is the one that we have been recreating each day, and that is largely responsible for what we have or have not allowed into our lives. Those of us who choose to walk through this gate are afforded the opportunity to truly create something new for ourselves.

The Dreamer Awakens

Before we begin our preparations I would like you to consider this thought. We are about to start the process of awakening from a long slumber, in which we have been dreaming our own version of reality. In this reality, maybe our world is in chaos and has become a very frightening place to live. Terrorists have attacked the United States and countless other countries around the globe, our dollar is plunging and with it our standard of living. Murder and all manner of crime greet us every time we turn on the TV. We are faced with "Global Warming" on one hand and on the other an economic model that is dependent on fossil fuels.

We have become so polarized as a nation that there is virtually no bipartisan support on major issues such as health care and immigration. Whether you are a Republican, a Democrat or a member of a growing body of independents, you may feel equally disappointed by the lack of direction and leadership that has been forthcoming.

The sad truth is that we have allowed our political system to be hijacked by corporate lobbyists and special interests! Using money and clout, including post-political job offers for our elected officials, ensures that cronyism runs rampant at the expense of the citizens they were elected to serve. The recent Citizens United court case has opened the flood gates to unprecedented individual and corporate influence of our elections, and the power of money as free speech was recently put to the test in Wisconsin's recall of Republican Governor Scott Walker, making him the first governor in U.S. history to survive a recall election.

In a 2010 Gallup Poll, some 57 percent of Americans view campaign donations as a protected form of free speech, and an even greater number believe that limits on both individual and corporate donations should be set. Today there are no limits, and the 2012 elections became a battle of those with the deepest pockets. With a total of 6 billion dollars spent and more than 1 million TV ads aired, it was the most expensive election in our history. Another issue to consider is undeclared or so-called dark money that comes from groups or individuals, often from outside of the state. A recent Mother Jones article stated that 57 percent of Walker's funds came from out-of-state supporters. However you view this, you will likely agree that this money was a large component of Governor Walker's victory. You may also agree that money and the media that it buys has the ability to change minds. If this were untrue then consumers would resist buying products that advertisers spend billions to have them buy! They do this by appealing to that part of us that is dissatisfied and demands satisfaction.

This dissatisfaction is largely an unconscious feeling that seeks justification and resolution through the story we repeat to ourselves each day. This fabrication of reality that we cling to has a consistent theme, though the plot may vary according to our circumstances. Our conscious mind seeks resolution and marketers of consumer goods or political agendas provide subplots that involve easily digestible solutions to our malaise. The truth is that we seldom vote consciously and that most of the gibberish coming out of politicians' mouths is designed to evoke our unconscious drives. Both parties are adept at this, though one has a much greater understanding of how to select a splinter issue and use it to garner support for a much broader agenda.

Cleverly crafted messages serve to emotionally arouse us while misdirecting our anger and frustration at the expense of much-needed resolution-based dialogue. Those of us with no real comprehension of the underlying issues become die-hard opponents of change that may in fact be in our best interest.

Anyone willing to check their facts will find that this country has undergone an unprecedented wealth shift over the past forty years. The middle class is fast disappearing, and those of us old enough still remember a country on the gold standard where couples could raise a family on one income. Now it takes two people each working forty hours a week or more to do the same. That is assuming that both of them have remained employed through this last economic downturn.

I Am Not Insane, I Just Don't Like Change!

It is little wonder that we may find ourselves tearing up over some tragic incident that occurs halfway around the world while a few minutes later we lash out angrily at our neighbor over some petty grievance. We as a culture are slipping into unconsciousness.

We are entertainment junkies, overfed, over drugged both legally and illegally and undernourished physically and spiritually. Let's not forget that this has all been accomplished by racking up our credit cards and putting second mortgages on our now-upside-down homes.

Our once industrious nation has now become a nation of debt serfs who are indentured to the money lenders. In a word, we are a culture in pain, and the sad part is that we have come to accept this as normal everyday life. We have been repeating these same behaviors over and over again with an expectation of a different result! It looks a lot like the definition of insanity to me. If we truly wanted change in our personal as well as our political environment we wouldn't be stuck in this ongoing cycle of disillusionment, fear and anger. We as individuals and as a nation have the ability to determine our fate. To do so we must be willing to step inside the wheel of life and then join with others in creating and unfolding a new vision for ourselves and our country.

It's Okay to Feel as It Leads to Awareness

Whether or not you agree with this picture that I have painted, my only hope is that you feel something. If you don't, the following statement may help you get there. It is our abnegation of personal responsibility that has placed us in this dilemma. I want you to feel the impact of our collective inaction and prepare you for where I am headed next.

Whose Story Is It, Anyway?

The significance of the above scenario is in the phrase "our own version of reality" and also in our reaction to it. The above statement is offered as a litmus test that will effectively trigger as many responses as there are readers. Even though we often imagine that others see the world the way that we do, that premise is false. Each of us views the world through our own unique set of filters put in place by a lifetime of experiences and our responses to them. Whether you are in agreement with, or repulsed by, the above scenario, take the feeling that you have and use it as an entry point into you own personal story. Then begin to write your story, the one that describes the who, what, where, when, and how of your current existence. Where is the why, you might ask? It is not very useful in this context, as it always demands justification!

From Cesspool to Resource Pool

Writing these personal stories is about acceptance of where we are right now in all areas of our lives. Whenever we feel a why coming on, an opportunity is presented for us to re-frame our past experience into a valuable resource. I am not suggesting that this is an easy task, though the end result may be new understandings about ourselves and how we choose to view the world. The very things that mired us in a life that appeared bleak and undesirable, when viewed from another perspective, may now become resources that will assist us as we begin to unfold our new path.

Emptying Your Cup

Doing this involves a practice of detachment from the old story, which then allows us to begin the act of opening to something new. The curious part of this procedure is that the form is circular. One cannot begin the process of detaching from this old story and all of its attributes without first accepting it. Many of us are so involved in repeating our story both internally and externally that we may not even be aware that we are doing so. Another scenario finds us pushing off from this old story in an attempt to disprove or deny it; then we must become conscious of it and embrace it fully, before we can release it. Whether defending or denying the old story on either a conscious or unconscious level, we are in effect indentured to it and unable to escape its grasp!

Making Room for Abundance

It is this fact that confuses and frustrates those of us who attempt to manifest abundance in our lives without first asking what having it will do for us. In most cases all we are doing is adding fuel to the karmic fires, and even if we were to somehow attract wealth it would probably be short lived, or at best less than fulfilling. This mechanism of wealth seeking is nothing more than the spirituality of greed, wrapped in a shiny new package. Abundance is and always has been available to each and every one of us, and to truly receive we must step modestly into the circle with our gifts.

It is usually this old story that we have been running from throughout our lives that holds us back from truly living. It is truthfully not more money or security that we are seeking, it is a life well lived that we desire. What is this well-lived life of which I speak? It is one lived with Duty, Devotion and Purpose. Without these fundamentals, we will never fully mature into adults, who then walk with Courage, Conviction and Strength.

When we as individuals make the choice, to dig down inside of ourselves and embrace this old tale, we may bear witness to the effects this narrative has produced on our lives. This knowledge will aid us on the journey back to being responsible, contributing members of our community. It is not possible to be a part of anything as long as we are still defending what is really no more than a concept of who and what we are! This clinging to a false identity is what prevents us from truly living life! This involves stepping outside of the prison that each of us creates for ourselves and onto the path of freedom that is our birthright.

Facing the Bear

In the medicine tradition as taught by Ten Bears, the bear represents courage and strength as well as playfulness. The bear is the most feared as well as being among the most playful of the creatures in the forest. The bear dwells in the west in the version of the medicine wheel that I learned, the eagle is in the east, the coyote the south and the white buffalo the north.

I was instructed to pray with intention to receive the teaching that spirit presented to me in my third year of Vision Quest.

Sitting in a sequester that is cramped, dark and hot during the day and pitch black and cold at night gives one the opportunity to face all kinds of fears. It was mid-afternoon of the second day and I felt supported by the sound of drums a short distance away as I completed a cleansing ceremony, raising the smudge bowl over my head, "Show me my path, Grandfather, and give me the courage to follow it!"

This prayer was the expression of my intention to face my fears and to open to my life path. It was not a new prayer for me, but it was one whose meaning I would soon embrace.

The sequester was round, made of a willow frame, bound together with twine and covered in black plastic and blankets. I was sitting cross-legged, my head was inches from the top and I could touch the side if I stretched out my legs. I was facing east towards the door, which had been sealed from the outside the previous evening. I had entered through a runway draped in prayer flags after being ceremoniously returned to spirit by my teacher Ten Bears.

This was my third year of a four-year commitment, and my thought was, I'm prepared for what spirit might invite in. I had spent the past year tying tobacco ties, some 750 of them, and after two previous Vision Quests I felt calm and focused. The previous year I had faced my fears when I heard a snorting sound outside the enclosure and recognized that it was a bear. I did feel fear grip my chest but had remained silent and after what seemed like an eternity it had moved on.

It had grown hot inside the enclosure and some time passed as I continued my prayers. I heard a rustling sound outside as something walked around the enclosure. That is when the snorting began and my heart started pounding. I told myself it would be okay and that it would soon go away just like last year. It was quiet for a moment and then the sequester shook! This was different, but I still remained hopeful until the enclosure was rocked fiercely a second time. My decision was made in that instant and on the third attempt, as claws tore through the plastic, I let out a yell from the pit of my belly while banging my boots together with my hands. I charged out to confront the bear who was down on all fours about fifteen feet from me. I grabbed a rock from the side of the enclosure and struck it in the flank. It turned and moved back another thirty feet and turned back towards me. The drummers who were not far away now approached and the bear yielded.

I crawled back into the sequester and was soon informed that my Vision Quest was complete and that Ten Bears wanted to see me. He invited me to sit with him and he congratulated me saying, "It looks like you have found what you were seeking?" I agreed and he said, "You have faced your fears and your medicine name is Standing Bear, get yourself a pipe and we will awaken it!" I became a pipe carrier that day and am honored to be called by the name "Standing Bear." I had faced my fears and was now fully committed to the process of becoming a human being!

Here I am using as an example the Vision Quest teaching of Ten Bears and his own expression of the traditional medicine path. The bear is truly something that we must face daily on our journey to awareness. It could come in the guise of a bully in your home, school or work life. It could also come as racism or sexism or any manner of prejudice, though most likely it will linger at your doorway as a presence waiting to be activated by some mostly unconscious story from your past.

There is a big difference between subjective and objective fear. One is in the mind, and the other one is clearly in front of you and must be dealt with as in the case of the bear. They both feel real to us, though it is the more common variety, subjective fear, which causes the most harm. It is constantly triggered by a hardwired, protective mechanism that wreaks havoc with our lives, as it has not evolved to cope with our modern world.

Most of us live in an uninterrupted cycle of subjective fear, and are simply unaware of its source or how to deal with it. This fight-or-flight response floods our bodies with powerful steroids and stimulants that keep us in a state of arousal that seeks an outlet. As an example, the fight response may be expressed as angry, disruptive behavior, and the flight response may be manifested as negative self-nurturing in the form of substance abuse, including food behaviors, drugs or social isolation through excessive gaming or television viewing.

The real damage occurs as these behaviors link themselves to our personal narrative and we lose ourselves to it, becoming unwitting participants in our own fabrication. The more we are willing to acknowledge these stories for what they are, the less power they have over us. Worrying about a future event is unproductive and the past is resolved not by constantly rehashing it, but by living into our new story, one that we create each day through the choices that we make.

The rest of this book is about just that. We will soon open the Toolbox and begin to explore with it, setting in place the consistency in our behaviors that is required to create the lives that we desire. Let us begin with the formulation of the invitation to this new life that we have chosen to unfold.

14. An Invitation To The Path Of Freedom

Where is the path of freedom, and what does it look like? Let me begin by saying, take a deep breath in, exhale and look around you, because this is your path. Where you are standing right now is the gateway to this path, and every step you take on it will determine the fruits of your journey. The path is within the "sacred wheel of life" and to enter this gateway we must each create our own invitation. This statement may be surprising to those of us who stood outside the door for many years, waiting for someone to invite us in while unaware that the gate was in fact open. This is the remarkable truth that I trust you will put to good use as you choose to tread upon this path.

Receiving and Accepting Your Invitation

The rest of this book is dedicated to the discovery and the unfoldment of each of our gifts. Through the utilization of the Primal Toolbox, we have the opportunity to become fully engaged in this process and reveal to ourselves a strength that will carry us into a purposeful life. The first exercise in the creation of your invitation begins with asking: What is it that I would have for myself, if nothing were holding me back from having it?

We Speak It into Existence on a Fully Sensory Level

Some of us are afraid to actually speak aloud, or declare what we would like our lives to be like. There are many reasons for this behavior and you are certainly welcome to fill in the blanks, though the only one that holds water is the following: Speaking out or declaring our desires conflicts with our old story, the one that we have been telling ourselves all of these years. The harboring of these unspoken hopes and desires may lead us to express things in a sideways manner that only serves to push us further from our goal. It is only when we are willing to begin the process, by releasing the old story, that we will make room for something new.

What Does Fully Sensory Mean?

The body translates and stores information on a sensory level, and the more our senses are involved the stronger the impact. Fully sensory means being totally engaged with all of our sense faculties! If we wish to create a future that is real for us, one that the subconscious mind will track and unfold, we must load it with sensory data. Tribal people do not merely think about what they wish to unfold, they transport themselves to a probable future and live into it as though it is already their reality. Creating your vision with this degree of intention ensures that it will unfold! Now imagine an individual, then a group, or even a nation doing so and the possibilities are enormous.

The Form Is Scalable

This process is equally valid whether being enacted by an individual, corporation or community (tribe). The simplicity of this form allows us to scale up the individual process with the only additional step being that of a convener (leader). The leader will present her view of the current situation (the old story). Even corporations live and die in relation to the stories that are repeated within their tribes each day. Nostalgia is a great panacea but it surely won't help an individual or a business to move forward. We are now witnessing a sea change in which entire business models are ceasing to exist. Many of yesterday's category crushers are today either gone or struggling to remain relevant. The details of the demise of these giants is well documented by Seth Godin in his books *Tribes* and *Linchpins*. He states that many of those industries will survive only by being willing to embrace a shift in their business model.

This shift is more difficult than most imagine, though not impossible. What were the stories that were being circulated at Kodak for the ten years before they went bankrupt? What of Blockbuster and their inability to embrace online streaming in its infancy? What of the Netflix fiasco in their handling of customers who were reluctant to embrace their new business model and still wanted CDs mailed to them? All of these situations could potentially have been avoided through the use of the following age-old techniques.

As a strong leader the CEO creates an Intentional Outcome. She then uses it to mobilize the company (tribe) in the creation of a new vision and story — one that is outcome based and fully sensory. The power of this exercise is enormous and combines the elements of storytelling and a vision quest. This is a positive and effective way to move your entire enterprise (tribe) in a new direction.

Right Use of Intention Begins with the End in Mind

Intention is the key to the universe! I am stating this as clearly and precisely as I am able, as I want you to understand the power that each of us has at our disposal. Understand that intention is always operating, and in most of us it does so on an unconscious level. Acknowledging this begins the process of opening us to the path of freedom.

It is the harnessing and directing of this intention that will enable us as individuals and as a society to begin to see that we are limitless beings who live in various sized "reality boxes" by intention (choice). True intention expressed consciously is transformational, and it has the power to awaken and inspire others. This requires a practice that fosters the daily renewal of Duty, Devotion and Purpose. When first utilized, intention will be only as effective as the practitioner that wields it. Like a dull tool it must be cared for and sharpened before each use. It must be stored appropriately and used judiciously in order to yield results.

Ancient Tools that Have Stood the Test of Time

This is a form that has a proven track record of many thousands of years and whose elements are now beginning to be utilized in groundbreaking techniques, by those willing to summon the courage to step outside of the box of their particular specialty.

When each of us chooses to define and categorize human beings based on narrowly constructed models of behavior, we miss the point. In doing so we fail to see the being who is reaching out to us from their own version of reality. It is only through the willingness to get some on us, to open our hearts to another that the real work gets done.

Each of us is shaped, not by the authority vested in us by another, but by the fearlessness required to search within until each of us discovers our truth. Those willing to do so will find that this truth is one of connection and creativity that needs approval from no one.

The success of these rituals is entirely related to the ability to create an intention that is strong enough to propel the individual or group past their egos, and into an entirely different experience. This effectively opens the individual or group to the freedom and possibility that is the natural state of the being. A shift has occurred in which our fear-based self-imposed boundaries have shifted to make room for something new. The more that we allow the unfettered mind to assume its rightful role of guiding us, the more passionate and fulfilled our lives become. The clinging to conformity that our modern society fosters leaves us little room to discover who we truly are.

The Edge of the Abyss

Ten Bears was laughing joyfully as he instructed his apprentices to let go. I stood transfixed, immobilized by fear, as I watched Michael Hoffman take a stride towards the edge of the cliff. Now running at full speed he spread his arms and disappeared. Time stood still and even Bart's laughter ceased for a moment. Then Michael appeared, ran by me, and jumped again! This was repeated several more times before I awoke in a sweat. Michael in my dream was showing me how to deal with my fears. The message from my unconscious mind was about repetition of danger! The more we challenge our fears, as Michael demonstrated in the dream, the easier it becomes to do so.

My inner consciousness was prompting me to step through the door or quite literally to jump into the abyss. This dream came to me at a time when I was considering a career change from a job that was steady, though not satisfying, to something that felt far more risky. Not long after that dream I summoned the courage to jump boldly into a new field of work, one that aligned with my life's purpose.

Risk-Free Change?

I had planned on making this career change for some time, I just needed to have enough money to ensure that I was not putting myself at risk. I had invested in some stocks that were going to be the next big thing and was literally waiting for my gold mine to come in. "The mining play is complete and you are now rich" would be the news! You can do anything that you want to do and still have all of the security that your heart desires. That, of course, was a great fantasy.

It wasn't long before the news of a merger faded and my shares value plummeted. It was at that point that I took a really hard look at my life and decided that I had to follow my heart's desire no matter what. I sold my mining shares, quit my job and jumped into the abyss. I took the skills that I had acquired over my twenty years with Ten Bears, added some new ones, and stepped onto my path of working with people. I then experienced the most difficult year that I can remember. I challenged all kinds of beliefs about myself and my capabilities, and by the end of that year, my life had been transformed.

Nobody Said that it would be Easy Living Out West

This statement was voiced by Ten Bears more than twenty years ago. It was his homey reply to his students' constant complaints about the difficulties encountered on our journey towards clarity. Most of us expected that it would be easy, and viewed our relationship with our teacher in terms of what he was going to give us. I and many of my cohorts were starting from a place of spiritual entitlement, though most were not consciously aware of this belief.

Entitlement on any level is a crippling behavior that breaks the natural cycle of abundance that is available to all. Tribal cultures had no tolerance for this attitude and members, typically as young children, would soon outgrow it. We now live in a society that fosters this behavior from birth to death and at every socioeconomic level. We are in the throes of a cultural tantrum with a vast number of factions fighting over what is perceived as an ever-diminishing piece of the American dream.

Entitlement Really, Really Sucks!

No really it does! It is what held me back from stepping into and owning my life's experience for so many years. My family didn't quite live up to my expectations; in fact no one did. As pathetic as this now sounds, it was a pretty big part of my operating system for a whole lot of years. Needless to say, it kept me in a state of dancing outside of "the wheel of life." It was also a mechanism that prevented me from challenging my fears and taking the action necessary to create the life that I desired.

Life Isn't Fair, It's Just Life

If you are looking for fairness you will find yourself sorely disappointed, because nothing is fair. This is a poorly understood premise that always accompanies entitlement. It is easy to feel that things are unfair when entitlement is your storyline. What each of us is entitled to according to the preamble to the Declaration of Independence is life, liberty and the pursuit of happiness, and these are unalienable rights. We hold these truths to be self-evident and unalienable, meaning that they are innate in the being, given at birth and not to be modified in any way, shape, or form.

What Is the Pursuit of Happiness?

Some would look at this and say that our forefathers were in favor of entitlement and use it to reinforce a "more is better, consumption rules" dictum. Others may use it to reinforce their belief in a free lunch, dinner, rent and retirement. When viewed through the eyes of detachment, these are opposite sides of the same coin. Happiness appears to embody either a risk-free state in which we can do as we please without consequence, or a utopia where someone else is doing it for us. We would solve a huge piece of our societal malaise if we as a nation were to truly understand and engage in the pursuit of happiness.

The key to the sentence is in the word pursuit. This word denotes an action, whereas happiness is the culmination of that action. The founding fathers were well schooled in classic Greek and Roman literature and were being precise in the choice of the phrase. John Locke, a seventeenth-century British political philosopher, stated that governments are instituted to secure people's rights to life, liberty and property. The founding fathers were aware of this line of reasoning, though deemed that the statement was insufficient as it lacked an essential element. When Thomas Jefferson penned the Declaration Of Independence he favored the phrase "pursuit of happiness."

The pursuit of happiness contains a moral aspect that denotes an action to grow in virtue and in excellence. The task of the founders was to provide the rich, fertile soil and leave the rest up to us. This is a far cry from a belief in entitlement that so many in our culture now adhere to.

Tracing Entitlement to Its Source

The belief in entitlement is not unique, though it certainly has attributes that must arise very early in childhood. I stated earlier that this behavior would not have been tolerated in intact tribal cultures and this is where we need to begin. The term intact is used to identify tribes that are not reliant on outside assistance, as it is this loss of self-sufficiency that enables the seeds of entitlement to take root.

This behavior is so harmful to the integrity of the tribe that it is easily identified in the child and addressed before it becomes an entrenched personality trait. Acknowledging its roots as a normal function of the developing child is the first step to the implementation of a strategy to change it. In our culture we may at first find these traits amusing, or simply dismiss them as the terrible two's, while allowing them to grow unhindered.

Belonging is a Privilege

We are all born inside of the sacred or primal circle with a sense that we are connected to everyone and everything. As self awareness takes hold, so begins this feeling of separation which is a normal, healthy developmental phase. Following a strategy of setting and supporting acceptable boundaries will allow the child to feel safe while exploring their new world. These are then appropriately expanded to accommodate the child's continued development. This is also where it becomes important to begin to instill the ethics and mores that will give the child a foundation upon which to frame their character. Though discipline is an essential element of this process, it is delivered as an invitation to become a part of something larger than themselves. The child is supported to become an active and vital member of the family, clan or tribe through a demonstration of valued behaviors and practices. These core practices, along with the ethics and mores, are the elements that sustain the integrity of the tribe through countless generations.

This self-indulgent mechanism in our own society has grown slowly over the past few hundred years, and more rapidly since the end of the second world war. Though it has likely been a component of the downfall of all great cultures throughout history, my interest is in offering solutions rather than historical analysis. It is my belief that a single generation of self-aware parents hold in their hands the keys to transforming our nation and perhaps our planet. Parenting is perhaps the most difficult and least understood skill in our culture.

Let me add that most parents have at the very least the intention to raise a healthy, vital and productive child. The problem is that the instructions were largely forgotten as we moved from a strong community based on relationship to a society of more isolated individuals. Entitlement has now become so entrenched that we view others through a predominantly fear-based model of scarcity, and consequently teach our children to view the world as we do. It is up to us as individuals and as a culture to empower ourselves to raise children with an understanding that entitlement is a sickness and that living in fear is a choice, not a necessity.

During the time I have been working on the Primal Toolbox, I have watched our country and the world slide evermore precariously towards the brink of cataclysmic change. I have struggled to put into words what I know to be true in my heart, and I want to frame it in a way that invites all sides to recognize the part that we play in this unfolding drama. Let us begin with the understanding that we humans will coalesce into groups any time more than two of us are present. These groups are formed naturally, as we feel either a kinship with others who share our views or a fear of those who do not. This bonding together to oppose others is a rudimentary trait found in all people who utilized it for safety and protection.

This protective mechanism was only a small part of the collective experience of tribal people, though it did serve as an internally driven process for determining threats from either inside or outside the tribe. These mechanisms are as relevant in humans today, who will instinctively group together to fend off a threat.

There is a major difference today, in that the perceived threats are delivered most often via the media to individuals, who then align themselves emotionally with groups or tribes who now coalesce around a particular message. These may be broken down along political, economic and social lines, with elements contained within each of these becoming the focus of the tribe's message. The individual benefits by feeling that they are a part of something important, and gladly repeats this message that has been delivered by our media culture with devastating effectiveness.

This is a harnessing of our Unconscious Intention in a way that undermines the very foundations of our culture. Tribal people may have been appropriately cautious in dealing with others outside of their tribe, though seeking resolution of differences would always be of utmost importance. Not so today, where citizens inundated with messages of danger find themselves in a highly stressed state with a perceived lack of resources to deal with it. It is this perception that itself keeps us locked in a cycle of fear, our emotions easily manipulated by those who understand the subtleties of persuasion.

The path through this fog of Unconscious Intention is actually well marked by those who have traversed it previously. Those of us willing to practice living with Conscious Intention will find that the trail becomes a little clearer each day. More important, each of us who is willing to tread this path makes it that much easier for the next person to do so.

15. The Primal Toolbox

The rest of this book is dedicated to the reviewing and utilization of the tools contained within the Primal Toolbox. The Change Strategies presented are based on tribal models and are designed to guide individuals or groups through the process of transformation. The creation of an Intentional Outcome may be used in goal setting or to effect behavior change in individuals and groups. For your convenience a glossary is provided in the back of the book.

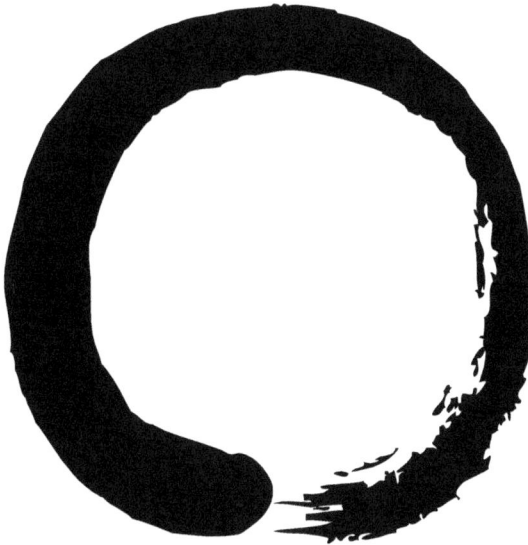

Let us begin by opening the toolbox and revealing the overall construct before we become more specific about its uses. Please note the diagram above in the form of a Zen circle. The circle represents the boundary between a life lived unconsciously and one lived with Conscious Intention. The interior of the circle is empty and paradoxically filled with possibility, while outside of the circle life is busy and chaotic, so full that it is bursting with limitation. The Zen circle is best viewed as an empty vessel into which we pour the makings of our new, more conscious life, and this begins with the creation of an Intentional Outcome.

The purpose of the toolbox is twofold. First it aids us in the setting, tracking and fulfillment of goals, whether personal or group oriented.

Second, we move progressively through the Four Stages of Awareness as we proceed to accomplish our goals. It is the linking of these processes that ensures that the desired change, having been arrived at consciously, will be lasting!

Please note that these stages are but a reflection of temporary states of awareness, and that all of us move back and forth between them on our journey towards the fourth stage. In the context of the Primal Toolbox, it marks our journey from a life lived unconsciously to a life lived with Conscious Intention. This life is arrived at through the harnessing of our Conscious and Unconscious Intention beyond the private interests of the individual and towards the goals of humanity. This development of a concern that is universal is the key element of an Intentional Core that fosters the Relational Excellence through which Conscious Stage Four Tribes evolve. The journey from a life lived unconsciously to a life lived with Conscious Intention begins as follows.

The Four Stages of Awareness

We begin our transformation process outside of the circle, dwelling in the land of the "accidental liver" as Ten Bears called it. This is the place of being at the effect of, rather than affecting our environment. This is a place of either crisis or complacency, a place filled with wishes and inaction. Planning is almost non-existent and we are often dependent on friends, family or the government to take care of our needs. Anger and frustration may be constant companions as the consequences of our behaviors are seldom linked to the behaviors themselves.

This is the place of entitlement that exudes a "life sucks" attitude, and groups that hang out here form tribes that share a similar world view. If you find yourself in this tribe, don't panic, as it may only be a temporary abode. Acknowledging that we are here prepares us for the journey forward. Also important to note is that these stages traverse all economic strata of society.

The language that is used here to describe each of these stages is derived from an outstanding book called *Tribal Leadership* by Dave Logan, John King and Haley Fischer-Wright. They produce a detailed analysis of successful corporate tribes and what it takes to create them. In their model they utilize a scale with five stages and identify tools that successful leaders implement to move through them.

They found that Stage Five Tribes are rare, composing less than 2% of workplace tribes. These are usually propelled to this state by an exceptional confluence of circumstances that are often summed up by the use of the word "miracle" to describe the experience. In the author's words, the emergence of Stage Five feels so unfamiliar that in describing it participants may go to religious or spiritual language to depict what has happened!

Though often dependent on extraordinary circumstances to achieve this cohesive state, these are actually glimpses into the possibilities of what in the Primal Coaching Model is a Conscious Stage Four Tribe. The "miracle" that is experienced is the "sacredness" that is a foundational attribute of a Conscious Stage Four Tribe. Let's take a closer look at the stages and how we may progress through them.

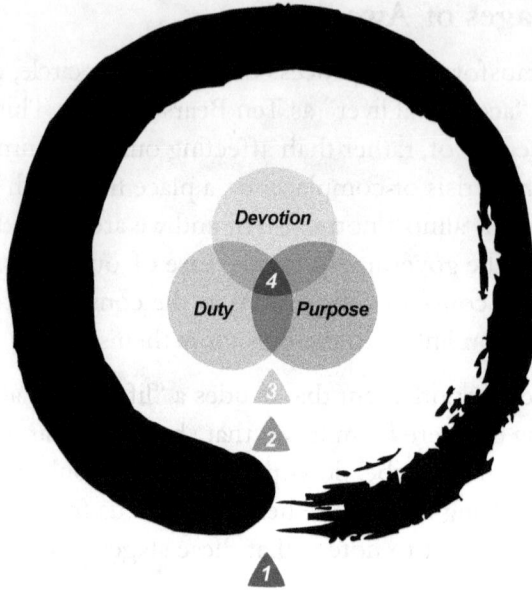

This First Stage of Awareness that I referred to is Unconscious Incompetence, and our movement from this stage, which is outside of the circle, is the beginning of our journey of awareness. Extricating ourselves from this stage is accomplished through entering one of two gateways, either hope or desperation. Though most of us choose desperation, either awakens us to the next stage, where we may begin to accept responsibility for our actions.

The circle is entered through the creation of Intention in the form of an Intentional Outcome that starts us on our journey of awareness. This Second Stage of Awareness is the start of our quest for personal or group transformation. This stage of Conscious Incompetence is the beginning of a movement towards self responsibility that is ignited by the willingness to look at the consequences of our choices. The language expressed here is appropriately "my life sucks." Identifying the language that constitutes our old story is a big step towards changing it. This is, in Ten Bears' vernacular, the "See how you are!" phase of understanding one's actions. It was his way of helping us to deduce that we are not our behaviors by telling us the opposite. This is an excellent example of the "Coyote medicine" he was so good at administering!

It is a difficult stage, as the tendency when confronted with our unproductive behaviors is to retreat into unconsciousness. These behaviors are governed by ineffective strategies that are reinforced by our personal or group story. The path to Conscious Awareness begins with the offering up of the old story and the creation of a new one that supports our Intentional Outcome. It is this new story in the form of a Transformational Tale that aligns with the key elements of our Intentional Core to effect the desired change.

An excellent example of an unconscious behavior being altered through the assistance of a feedback loop was offered in the June 2011 edition of Wired magazine. The incident being referred to took place in Garden Grove, CA, where repeated accidents were occurring in school zones due to excessive speed. Standard methods of ticketing and improved signage had limited effect and the city engineers decided to experiment with what at the time was a new technology. They put up dynamic speed displays in five area school zones that digitally displayed the drivers' speeds as they passed.

The results were excellent and drivers slowed down by an average of 14 percent, while three schools had average recorded speeds below the posted limit. Most people do not consciously intend to speed through school zones, or engage in so many other behaviors that are equally nonproductive; they are just doing so unconsciously. Next time you catch yourself speeding in a school zone and slow down, be thankful that you have just experienced the Second Stage of Awareness.

This is the stage of Conscious Incompetence, where we begin to become aware of our old behaviors and the beliefs that support them. This new-found awareness is the key as we are now presented with a choice! We can either face our old beliefs and move towards the third stage, or feel overwhelmed by them. It is the incremental nature of change that is most difficult to grasp. The truth is that lasting change is always arrived at through consistent daily application of Change Strategies that when followed will lead to desirable outcomes. Consistent action over time that is aligned with our Intentional Outcome produces results, and utilizing the Change Modules contained within the toolbox will assist us in tracking where we are in the process. This affords us the opportunity to make adjustments and stay on course as our life continues to unfold.

The next Stage of Awareness is Conscious Competence, where we begin to experience that sense of freedom that is born of personal responsibility. This empowering feeling comes from having put in place the limits that we have – up until now – resisted. These limits will vary according to the outcomes that we have selected to focus on. As an example, if it is our intention to have a long and prosperous life, then two easy areas to emphasize would be health and wellness, as well as fiscal planning. How many of us arrive at retirement with either one or both of these areas lacking? Success in both of these worthy aims involves placing limitations, in one case on our expenditures, and in the other case on food , including our food choices and the quantity of food that we eat, as well as perhaps limiting our hours on the couch.

Though these limits are put in place in the second stage, they become a practice in the third and begin to bear fruit. The new habits and behaviors that were seeded in the second stage are slowly beginning to take root in the form of a new personal story that is affirmed through our actions. The language of this stage is "I'm great" and is reflective of an individual's sense of accomplishment.

This final stage of Unconscious Competence is where we reap the benefits of our behavior changes and are living more productive and fulfilling lives. We operate from an Intentional Core and are now practicing with Conscious Intention while utilizing the Change Modules to insure that we are on track with our short-term goals as well as aligning with our life's purpose. This is the point of transformation to the Relational Excellence that is the foundation of a Conscious Stage Four Tribe. The language of this stage is a unifying "we're great," which is a building block of Relational Excellence.

The attitude that produces a Conscious Stage Four Tribe is one of encouraging members to discover and share their gifts. The people that accomplish great things within our American culture are celebrated as talented rebels, outliers that somehow break the mold. What if we lived in a society that encouraged excellence as a birthright? Without a foundation for the development of the principles of Individual Excellence we are left without a framework for the practice of Relational Excellence. The attributes of Individual Excellence when celebrated within a group will produce the fertile ground from which Relational Excellence and a Conscious Stage Four Tribe may grow.

The language of a Conscious Stage Four Tribe is "life is good," an expression of the gratitude that each member feels by way of acknowledgment of the acceptance of their contribution to the whole. This tribe or enterprise has evolved from a loose association of individuals, each fighting for their fair share, to a cohesive group who share a common vision and purpose. Most important, their concern is for the good of the whole, and each member counts themselves as "one of the people." This is a move from "I" to "We" consciousness and is the foundation of our Primal Nature.

It is this Primal Nature that is the missing element in our culture today, and the full utilization of these tools I am presenting is designed to open us to this experience. This is by no means an extraordinary state of consciousness; it is not some mystical stage of awareness or enlightenment. It is in fact a return to that which is our birthright, to a knowing that we have all experienced as children. It is a sense that we are part of something much greater than this body we are occupying during our short visit to this world. It is this knowing that we fall away from, and that creates a longing that we spend our lives searching to satisfy. It is this yearning that produces so much of the unhappiness we experience throughout our lives and is in turn the source of so many of our non-productive behaviors. We spend our lives trying to fill this void without understanding the metaphorical nature of our primarily unconscious actions. We have been engaging in these old habits and behaviors for a long time and can surmise that they are an attempt, though often inadequate or misguided, to meet our deep-seated needs.

It's a Love-Hate Relationship

In the Primal Coaching Model we recognize these behaviors for the limited strategies that they are, and when we cease to empower them they soon lose their grip on us! We do so by asking what it is that we truly desire for ourselves. Giving up these habits is a lot like walking away from a dysfunctional relationship. If we believe it's the only thing that we have, it can be difficult to let it go! Many of us are actually hesitant to ask for what we desire as we may feel that it is simply unavailable to us. That is, of course, what our personal story is telling us.

The Change Modules

Please note the Change Modules are located outside of the circle in the diagram, as their use reinforces our Intention Cycle. This cycle of directed intention acts as a feedback loop to keep us tracking our Intentional Outcome. The use of the modules each day insures that the recurrence of unconscious behaviors will become less frequent as they are called out into the light of conscious awareness. This is accomplished through the gathering of appropriately contextualized data that enables an actionable response based on choice.

The four Change Modules constitute one full cycle of directed creative action. This Intention Cycle is based on four transitional stages that provide the template upon which our intention may be nurtured, cultivated and received. Let's look more closely at what composes each of the modules.

The Creation Module

The Creation Module is where the transformation process begins to take shape! This is springtime, the eastern gate, and is where we prepare to enter the "sacred wheel of life" as depicted by the Primal Toolbox diagram. This action begins with the offering up of our old story, the one that has kept us in this cycle of limitation. The most important aspect is to be as honest as we can, to avoid blame, and to get in touch with the emotion that accompanies the experience. Once this old story has been identified, we will enact a releasing ceremony, thank it for the lessons and let it go. This can be accomplished in many equally effective ways from burning to burying; just bring your Conscious Intention into the form that you utilize.

Viewed from a Zen tradition, this process would be akin to emptying the cup and making room for something new. In the tradition of Ten Bears, it would correlate with the tying of red tobacco ties in preparation for a Vision Quest. The Creation Module is used initially to enter the circle, as well as daily with the three other modules to keep us tracking our dream. This daily reaffirmation process is important, for without it we may lose our focus and soon find we are hesitant to even acknowledge that we have a dream, as doing so would give cause to reflect on how far we have strayed from it.

The art of dreaming has been lost in our culture, or rather relinquished to the high priests of marketing who are only too happy to provide one for us. This book is about reactivating our ability to dream big dreams and to share them as our contribution to the ocean of creativity that is the human tribe.

The same principles that we activate to create our larger vision and purpose are equally effective in putting in place the goals that we use to guide our daily actions. It is this process of sustained action over time that ensures the unfoldment of our dream. Creating this vision or dream begins with a process of expansion. We simply let our imagination go and begin to envision ourselves in the dream doing that which we desire. If we are uncertain of what that is, then we simply allow ourselves to try on different ideas until something resonates with us. This exercise is all about possibility, thinking and allowing ourselves to see, hear and feel it from within, to simply let our excitement build. This process is enacted over time and could take days, weeks or months to refine itself into a vision worthy of our directed action.

An Intentional Outcome Sets the Parameters

This expansion of possibilities is often accompanied by an urge to immediately quit what we are doing and pursue this full time without adequate preparation. This, as you would guess, is not a grounded approach and will most likely leave us at risk. It is now time to utilize our tools and create a plan in the form of an Intentional Outcome. This new-found feeling is the beginning of a transformational process that is first allowed to expand, and then pulled back in until it fits all of the parameters of our Intentional Outcome.

The harnessing and directing of our energy through the creation of an Intentional Outcome will enable us to transition into our new dynamic, with all of the resources that will ensure our success! Now we check our desired outcomes alignment with our Intentional Core, and explore its probable future to ensure its unimpeded unfoldment. The seeds of success are now sown and begin to take root.

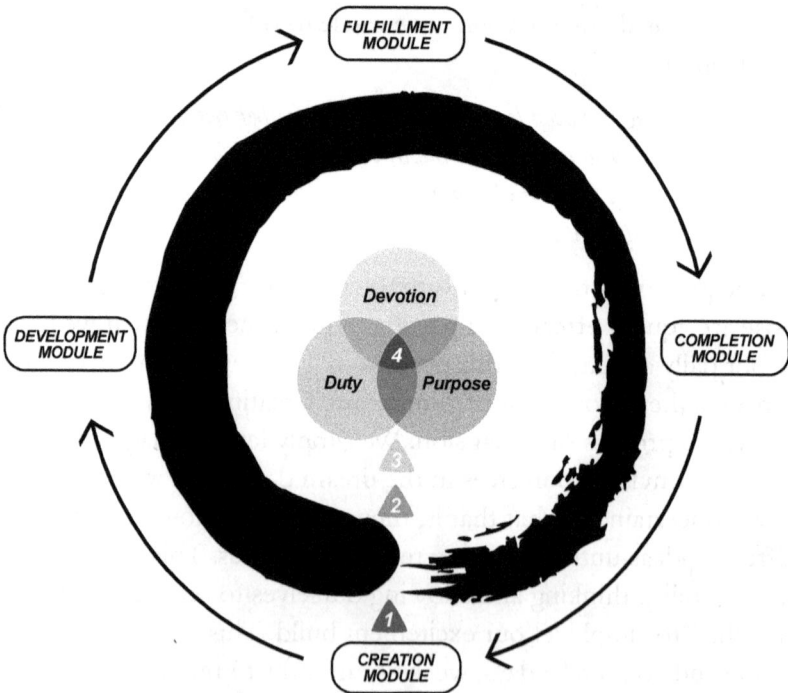

Before we move on to the other change modules, let's look more closely at the Intentional Core and how its utilization provides the elements that will insure that the outcomes we are seeking are achieved. It is this core around which our commitment is activated and sustained through our daily renewal of it. This center forms itself around the three primary attributes of Duty, Devotion and Purpose and ensures that actions originating from here align with our Intentional Outcome. Over time these primary or adolescent attributes become internalized and transformed into the adult attributes of Courage, Conviction and Strength. Our fully matured Intentional Core is in effect, evoking what we stand for as individuals or as a group.

The Intentional Core – Formative

This Intentional Core is the missing template that supports a model for healthy human behavior in today's world, and without it, we spend our time shoring up temporary structures that inevitably fall down around us. Without an intact Intentional Core we are constantly at the effect of our emotional states and their associated behavior patterns. It is only through our willingness to let go of these old state dependent patterns that we can begin to create something new.

Let's look more closely at the primary elements that are contained within the core and how we may utilize them in our daily practice of awareness.

Duty. A moral commitment that results in action that is directed towards a cause. This is done from a view beyond limited self interest. It is activated from concern for the greater good, and directed from a deep understanding that duty is an offering of our gift to another, to our tribe or society. Most important, it is a debt that we owe ourselves as human beings. To freely give of ourselves opens us to the rich, full and abundant life that we desire and deserve.

Devotion. A consistent action over time towards a cause. This creative force contains the idea of duration both in and beyond time. It is a movement that never stops or slows, just as one day leads to another in an unending passage of time. The goal itself is already realized unconsciously. All that is required is the conscious unfoldment of it. Effort that springs from the certainty of this unconscious realization is resolute action.

Purpose. That which gives meaning to our actions. It is the intentional offering of our gifts that in return actualizes them. This little-understood dichotomy is the wellspring of all good in human relations. This single element creates in the being a state of joy.

These primary attributes and their utilization in conjunction with the Change Modules will aid us in our transformation into a new dynamic. The non-productive behaviors that were once used to justify and reinforce our old story now become our offering to the fires of self awareness. This practice of Conscious Intention over time forms the foundation for a new way of interacting with our world.

Intentional Core – Mature

The shift that occurs is as dramatic as a new birth, and is celebrated in tribal cultures as a rite of passage. It is nothing less than a shift from an adolescent world view to that of an adult. We have coalesced our diverse energies around a fully formed Intentional Core and no longer look outward to define ourselves. We have turned our gaze inwards and now act with a strength that has been tested. This is the beginning of our walk as an integrated and resourceful human being. We are now unfolding the adult attributes of Courage, Conviction and Strength.

Courage. The ability to stand up or face danger, fear, or intimidation at risk of physical pain or threat of death. It also has a moral component that enables one to stand in their truth and defend it through speech or action. This was referred to by Ten Bears as being the "requiredness of the situation."

Conviction. Standing with and acting from a certainty or belief that ensures our actions align with our truth. This is the source of resolute action.

Strength. The folding and welding of pieces of high and low carbon steel in a Samurai sword or Katana, combined with rapid cooling, create a strong yet flexible weapon. It is this tensile strength achieved through repeatedly testing the steel that provides the metaphor for strength. It is through repeated testing that one acquires the fortitude, power, potency and expertise that are the qualities representative of true strength.

Now that we have reviewed the Intentional Core and its attributes we will return to the Change Modules and take a closer look at how they serve as a feedback loop to keep us tracking our Intentional Outcome.

The Development Module

The Development Module is the second of the four and acts as a resource center where skills and materials are gathered, refined and applied as we unfold our Intentional Outcome. This is the place of the south and coordinates with summer on the "sacred wheel," the season of growth and activity. It is here that we direct our actions with all of our intention in order to take full advantage of the energy of the moment. All endeavors have a natural flow to them and when we honor this cycle, we will be renewed by it.

This module fosters action over time that is directed in the form of an offering towards an Intentional Outcome. This requires the full utilization and consistent application of one's resources, undeviating from our Intentional Core. It is this gift of our energy in the form of Duty, Devotion and Purpose that moves our actions from the mundane into the sacred. This is done with the knowledge that the desired result is awaiting us and that all that is required is consistent action day in and day out in the form of our Individual Excellence.

Generating An Intention Cycle

The use of the modules each day in this practice of Individual Excellence generates an Intention Cycle that serves as a feedback loop. We are now able to see more clearly, how closely our actions align with our Intentional Core, as well as the consequences of our actions when they fail to do so. As movement through the Stages of Awareness continues, the recurrence of unconscious behaviors becomes less frequent, as we are now honing our ability to become more conscious of them. It is this ongoing interaction with the Change Modules and our Intentional Core that will ensure the realization of our Intentional Outcome.

The influence of the Change Modules is one of reminding us of how resourceful we truly are as well as how capable we are becoming. In tribal cultures this role is fulfilled by the elders, who mentor the younger members of the group each day until these skills become second nature. Then, each evening members gather around the fire and share stories that reflect the ethics and mores that constitute their Intentional Core as well as their Operational Core. This process is an act of love that passes the skills from one generation to another, but, more important, also reinforces the significance of the individual's contribution to the group. It is this development and alignment of each member's Intentional Core with that of the group's Operational Core that was the most sacred of occurrences. This was celebrated and acknowledged in a way that encouraged and rewarded this Relational Excellence.

The Fulfillment Module

The Fulfillment Module equates with fall, on the "sacred wheel" the place of the west, and it is here where we receive the results of our labor. Though it is easiest to view these modules as an annual cycle with their correspondence to the seasons, that would be true only in the broadest sense. It is their function that we are addressing here as well as their utilization in the form of an Intention Cycle. This cycle is applicable over multiple time frames from days, weeks, and months to years, or may simply be used to track the progress of a task.

When we look at the term fulfillment and we see it as primarily the accomplishment of a task, we are missing a much deeper level of expression. What is easily overlooked in our frenzied, results-driven culture is our state of realization of that completion. It is an expansive feeling of satisfaction, of joy, and of abundance that is felt by the individual at this time of fulfillment. This is fruition, the natural unfolding of potential in nature and in man.

This is the place of receiving; that which flows from our consistent action over time. The desired result is apparent as we are now bearing witness to the fruits of our labor. This is the time of harvest, of making full use of this period of abundance. It is also a time of celebration, of acknowledging all the effort that was directed towards this end. In the context of a tribe, this festivity is a communal ceremony that gives thanks to Individual Excellence as a natural expression of Relational Excellence.

Practicing Awareness Yields Results

In acknowledging that our actions always bear fruit, we now place our focus on the level of awareness with which we choose to engage our world. It is our lack of attention to this causality that leaves us feeling frustrated with our results. Unconscious acts arising in the First Stage of Awareness produce unintended consequences, whereas unconscious actions arising in the Fourth Stage of Awareness are aligned with our Intentional Outcome. In the first case, unproductive behavior patterns and their associated emotional states leave us mired in unconsciousness, often feeling isolated and alone. In the second our now productive behavior patterns are operating in a way that supports our Individual and Relational Excellence. This is the alpha and omega of our quest to master the behaviors that keep so much of our awareness and vital energy locked up.

The inconsistency of our conduct in the Second Stage of Awareness produces conflicting results that may leave us in a less or more resourceful frame of mind. This is dependent upon the criteria as well as the emotional state through which we filter our experiences. The following is an example of how the process may unfold.

If we create an Intentional Outcome to change a behavior and in the Second Stage of Awareness, by bringing more attention to our behavior, discover that we have just engaged in it, we may be disappointed in ourselves. Keep in mind that behavior change is both cyclical and state dependent! What is meant by that phrase is that a positive choice made, in turn helps us to more easily make more positive choices. That sounds great! Except for the fact that a negative choice made may help us make more negative choices.

It's Time to Change Your Filter

It is this aspect of the change cycle that will empower us to use the Change Modules to shift our strategies as we begin to understand this mechanism. How can the same behavior be viewed so differently by the same person at different times? It is, after all, just a behavior, isn't it? If that is the case, why do we feel so poorly at times when we catch ourselves in a non-productive behavior? This is where state dependence and criteria come into play. The emotional state we are in while engaging in behaviors and the criteria we use to judge them regulate how resourceful we determine the experience to be.

This is where things can get tricky. If the metric with which we judge them is filtered through our old story, we may justify the behavior or we may despise it and ourselves for engaging in it. We could also find ourselves engaging in negative self-talk that springs from an emotional state that reinforces our perceived failure to change this behavior. This is the most difficult stage, as we are now having to confront our old story – the one that has supported and justified our non-productive behaviors.

The use of the Change Modules will assist us in detaching from expectation and perfection, as these serve no one. Focusing instead on the foundational practice of Individual Excellence, we become more adept each day as we put in place the behaviors that will carry us into the Third Stage of Awareness, which is Conscious Competence.

It is our more congruent initiative in the Third Stage that, when consciously sustained, will over time move us into the Unconscious Competence of the Fourth Stage of Awareness. It is in this stage that our unconscious actions are now aligned with our Intentional Outcome and we are living the abundant life that we desire and deserve. The feeling is one of being unfettered, as our minds and bodies are freed from the heavy expenditure of energy that we have been using just to maintain our lives. We have succeeded in bringing our awareness and intention together, consistently demonstrating how resourceful we truly are.

This is but the beginning of our journey, as our new-found awareness will continue to expand until it enters into every area of our lives. That very thing that caused us so much grief only a short time ago has now become a key to our transformational process.

The Completion Module

We are now going to look at the Completion Module, the fourth and final module, one that is so often overlooked in a world that is governed by today's non-sustainable, consumption-driven, continuous-growth model. We are so busy doing that we often fail to consider the results of our actions upon completion. The final stage is one of reflection and contemplation, of reviewing the effects of our action and asking, "Is what we have accomplished completely aligned with our Core Intention?" This practice is used at the end of projects or tasks to insure that all of the value of the experience has been gleaned and nothing left undone. This often-neglected element, when used daily, will assure that our actions are both sufficient and directed towards our Intentional Outcome.

Checking congruence as a practice keeps us tracking our Conscious rather than Unconscious Intention. The seasons of the year and their transition points provide tribal people with a template that marks this movement. When viewed as a passage, wherein the participants are borne along by nature, one begins to comprehend their relationship to it. It is this collaboration with nature that is less understood today as we move further from a direct experience of it. We do not have to be in the deep woods to connect to it; just turn off the iPod on our next walk or while sitting out in the yard, let go of our concept of nature, and let ourselves feel it.

In doing so we will soon discover that the day has transition points as do the seasons, the most obvious being sunrise and sunset, and these may be utilized to remind us of our Intentional Outcome through renewing it each morning and reviewing it each evening. Through reviewing our day or an individual task we are able to determine the degree to which we have either engaged in Individual Excellence or slipped into unconscious behavior patterns. It is this practice of introspection that keeps our intention from going astray.

This practice endured in more complex cultures such as ancient China, where it was customary to close the gates of the empire during the winter solstice for a ten day period of reflection and contemplation. People were encouraged to discard unproductive practices and begin the new year with a clean slate and renewed intention. This process of reviewing and then letting go of our conditioned or unconscious behaviors will make room for the change we desire. An ideal time to do this is prior to bedtime; it only takes a few minutes to get closure on our day and we may soon find that we are sleeping more soundly!

16. A Life of Freedom and Expression

The consistent use of the Change Modules over time creates an Intention Cycle that begins to feel more automatic, enabling us to pour more energy and passion into our Intentional Outcome. The old story that has supported our unproductive behaviors is becoming less dominant as we continue to unfold our new one. This is the freeing up of our Intentional Core and for all intents and purposes it feels like a rebirth. This is the state that Ten Bears encouraged with the words, "Add life to your living!"

This is the entryway into the Third Stage of Awareness and our shift from an unconscious reliance on our old story to a conscious enactment of our new one. This is an exciting time as we are now seeing the results of our consistent effort and feeling pleased at our achievement. Our newly acquired behaviors and practices are starting to bear fruit and it is at this point that we must remain vigilant. The act of focusing solely on the result may prompt us to put things on autopilot and begin to drift off course.

How can that happen you ask, and isn't it important to acknowledge our success? Yes, the recognition of this achievement is an important component of this change, but to make it lasting we must celebrate the actions that produced these results. It is important to clarify the difference between behaviors that are modified through an external stimulus and those that arise from our Intentional Core.

Boot camp is the perfect example to demonstrate the difference! How many who have served were in the best shape of their lives after basic training? Did this happen through intention or was it because of a butt kicking drill instructor? How long did the changes in fitness level last? For a small number of people the changes were permanent, but for most they slipped away over time.

Regimen vs. Self-Discipline

The difference between these two practices is the reason why diets and fitness programs usually fail. Following a rigid program to lose weight and get in shape, we begin working out, perhaps counting calories or points, or eating prepackaged food. We will have various degrees of success and a lot of resentment at having to do this! This externally activated process is regimen and will grudgingly induce a temporary change at best, which we equate with failure as it slips away. While being self-responsible produces a practice of Individual Excellence that opens us to a life of transformation, the difference between these two models for behavior change is the pivot upon which all change is hinged. Regimen is a largely unconscious practice, while self-discipline is activated through conscious intention.

Focusing purely on the result whether we view it as positive or negative is akin to paddling a canoe while facing backwards while your guide is calling out instructions to keep you on course. Arriving at the desired destination without having acquired any new navigational skills, we celebrate our success while bidding our guide farewell. This of course frees us to drift into the weeds along the shoreline of unproductive behaviors, a place that is to most of us all too familiar. We begin to neglect the very things that we have utilized to attain this level of success, and in doing so slip back into the First Stage of Awareness.

Turn Around and Paddle

An important aspect of the Change Strategies that are presented here is the discipline of focusing on what we want, not what we don't want! In doing so we begin to align with our new story and support it with our choices. Though that sounds simple enough, this practice involves letting go of the comfort of these old behavior patterns, many of which were put in place as children. While it sounds strange to associate comfort with behaviors that are leaving us with less than productive outcomes, the old adage, "We are creatures of habit," still holds true. Unfortunately, we identify ourselves as this "creature" that has all of the attributes of our habits and learn to despise the "creature" along with the habit.

Nothing Personal! It's Just a Habit!

It is this identification that keeps us locked into the old story. It is our story, after all, and we derive a degree of comfort from its predictability! The truth is that without having the support of a new story we will cling tenaciously to the old one. It is the use of the Change Modules, outfitted with all the tools needed, that enable this transformation to take place.

As stated above, these behaviors are put in place in childhood usually through our relationships with our parents and siblings. Once in place they are then reinforced by our interactions with our teachers, coworkers and our bosses. Blaming any of them is wasted energy, as they were likely just doing the best that they could with the information they had at hand. I am in no way excusing abusive or malicious behavior, just the general unconsciousness that comes from a lack of Relational Excellence. Without a template that encourages the development of both Individual and Relational Excellence within the family, we are ill equipped as we venture out into the larger community. It is from this murky environment that the creature originates and develops behaviors that support its beliefs.

Our inability to understand this broader picture is the root cause of our malaise and keeps us from addressing and resolving the issue. The "creature" is very real on an emotional level and must be fed or indulged to keep it alive! Changing our behaviors may feel as though we are killing a part of us! If that is the case, how will we ever change our behaviors? We do so by inviting the creature to arise from the murky depths and join with us in creating something different. This is accomplished through the creation of a new personal story that is supported by our action. This then becomes our Transformational Tale, our story of becoming! It is the acting out of our new story day by day that transforms the "creature" by way of Individual Excellence from an ogre to a prince.

Changing the Seeds

Each day of our lives we repeat a portion of our personal story to ourselves that reinforces our current state. This state is filtered through our emotions and supported by our beliefs, which in turn support our behaviors. These behaviors are in fact the result of a feedback loop that is operating on a largely unconscious level. This mechanism is supporting as well as being supported by our personal narrative. Seeds are sown and watered each day in the thought fields of our mind, yielding a stronger narrative and more behaviors. This wheel of the mind is Samsara, the karmic wheel that is spoken of in eastern religions. We create karma through unconscious actions and what people refer to as "bad karma" is in fact the effects of our mostly unconscious behavior patterns. This karma manifests in many forms, as our actions affect not only ourselves but others both directly and indirectly. These thought seeds are the key to our transformation process in that all of us recognize that inferior seed produces an inferior crop. How then do we change the quality of the seed to insure that a healthier crop is cultivated? The answer to this question is a key to the transformation process in individuals and groups.

The comparison of the subconscious mind to a computer's database is an often used attempt to simplify a complex process. While the idea of wiping a corrupted hard-drive and reinstalling new software sounds like an appealing way to clear up your computer problems, it doesn't really translate to the human mind. Another computer analogy does, however, appear to serve our understanding more accurately, and that is overwriting the data. This technique does translate to practices that have been utilized effectively by tribal people to communicate directly to the subconscious mind.

This communication takes place in the form of the constant storytelling that occurs both formally and informally among tribal members. The ethic and mores of the tribe are communicated from the elders to the younger members, which creates a shared story. This story is delivered on a conscious and subconscious level each day and is reaffirmed through the collective actions of the tribe. The repetition of this evolving story is the root of Relational Excellence and the "We" consciousness that is present in Conscious Stage Four Tribes. This constant retelling of the story by members is the overwriting of the data that insures the message is error free. Doing the same today by conventional means is anything but simple. Being born into a Conscious Stage Four Tribe is no longer an option for most of us!

Culturally we range across the whole spectrum and are skewed towards a stage two or three at best. We cannot blame ourselves, as this is the story that we have been handed down and that we are passing on to the next generation. We no longer possess a story of "who we are as a people" and as a result we stand for nothing. "Standing for something" is a practice that starts with our willingness to step beyond our limited self concept and begin to share from our heart. When we do so we find we are aligning with our life's purpose.

There is a story resonating within each of us that is being repeated by those who have heard it. Though it is being drowned out by the din of modern life, it can be heard by anyone who is willing to take the time to quiet their mind long enough to listen. Trust that this story is inherent in the being and will reveal itself over time, as it springs from our Primal Nature! It is beyond vocal resonance or even thought patterns and to describe it always leaves us wanting. It is a deep knowing that is felt equally by the Masai tribesman on the plains of Africa and the lone hiker witnessing a sunrise from a mountaintop in Washington State.

It is first and foremost a story of unity, with each other and with creation itself. It is the gateway to the infinite, the razor's edge upon which we tread, that will one day return us to the source. The circle of one that breathes the endless cycles of creation into existence.

Begin with a Trial Separation

This process of reconnecting begins with a willingness to let go of the background noise that has been masking this underlying story. This noise is both internal and external, though discerning the difference may at first seem difficult as this duet has been together for a long time. An effective practice is to limit external distractions for periods throughout your day by sitting quietly in an environment in your home that gives you permission, to relax. Create a space in which to sit and get in touch with the sacredness that is you. Choose elements that help you accomplish this, from candles and incense to prayer beads or anything else that has special meaning to you. Turn off your smartphone, TV, and iPod, and go gadget free for a period of time each day. You may find that you enjoy this new feeling of calmness. Sitting quietly is an unfamiliar experience to most of us, and it is normal to experience some discomfort as we begin this process of body-mind awareness.

Be patient with yourself, become curious about the sensations you are experiencing without judging them or pushing them away. You will soon discover your center, the space that nurtures and supports who you are as a being. This is the start to your journey home, a place that you will one day discover has always been much closer than you imagined!

From Mind-Heart to Heart-Mind

During the summer solstice ceremony of 2003 I came to the realization that I was in need of guidance, and made an offering to my teacher Ten

Bears with a request that he support me in a Vision Quest. This was impromptu, as it had been several years since I had completed my four-year round that involved a year of preparation for each. Fortunately, he accepted, and finding a suitable location we got under way. I built a small enclosure, crawled in with my pipe and prayed throughout the night and next day. I was supported by Ten Bears and fellow apprentice Michael Hoffman, whose prayers gave me strength.

It was late afternoon by now and a battle was raging inside of me. I was overcome by a thirst that was more than physical, combined with a knowledge that this Vision Quest would soon end. Singing and rattling with all the energy I could muster, supported by Michael drumming, I lost track of time. The drumming stopped and I heard footsteps walking towards me when it happened. I summoned one last burst of song and felt energy rise from the base of my spine and shoot up through the crown of my head; the feeling of relief was enormous.

Ten Bears invited me to re-enter the world and I did so crawling out on all fours. I could barely stand without assistance. I felt so free and expansive that I knew I could do just about anything, and that is when the ego took hold and declared just that. The most hideous comment came out of my mouth and I did not even acknowledge it until Ten Bears later addressed it. It was a lust filled statement of arrogance that exemplified the worst aspect of my male programming. I was entitled to have any woman I desired and the one I desired at that moment was far from available. I was soon so embarrassed by this outburst that I despised the part of me that uttered it. I regret that I never sorted this out with my teacher, as it would have saved me years of remorse. At the very moment I experienced this awakening I was puking out unconscious behavior patterns and unrealized desires.

I lay down in the stream and let the water rush over me, though it felt more like it was flowing through me. After Ten Bears' offer of water and some fruit, my strength slowly started to return. We packed up camp and headed back to Boise where I would catch a plane and fly to southern Utah to spend a few days with my brother before returning to Dallas. We stopped at a restaurant on the river and sat outside in the courtyard and had dinner surrounded by some of the most astonishing people I had ever seen. They were all shapes and sizes and ages from young to old and

I was amazed at their beauty. Ten Bears asked me, "How is your world looking right about now?" All I could say was, "Beautiful!"

I am at that moment seeing the world as it is, without need to judge or filter it, and am in awe. Words fail to describe the experience, though the feeling is one of bearing witness, and yet there is no me to do so!

I would like to tell you that this expansiveness continued unhindered and I soon learned to dwell in this blissful state and beyond. Instead I clung to my shame and embarrassment over my statement to my teacher and a lifetime of associated behaviors. I was identifying myself through my past behaviors and the cost of this error was enormous. Over the next few months the energy dissipated and a huge opportunity to understand the experience was lost. With courage I could have embraced these behaviors and learned the lessons associated with them instead of trying to deny and bury them. I now understand them to be a sideways expression of my desire to love and be loved!

The biggest lesson that I walked away with was that it was time to wrap up my business in Dallas and choose a different path. At that moment I decided to accept my teacher's invitation to apprentice with him, and moved to Waitsburg, WA, where I spent the next 15 months learning some incredible lessons. Having worked with Ten Bears for 20 years until his death in July 2007, it was my time spent living with him that had the most profound effect on me. Everything he did was designed to help me discover the beautiful being that I am, though viewed through my filtered reality it was at times an aggravation that involved peeling back some layers that I really did not want to look at. He was asking me to be conscious of my behaviors as well as accept responsibility for them. I was in effect moving through the second stage of learning, and it was not pleasant.

We human beings operate with a heart-mind connection that is designed to process our experience in just this way. We take it in through the expansiveness of the heart and then filter it cognitively through the mind. Like many of us, I had learned at a young age to shut this connection down and filter things through the mind-heart. When we experience our world through the limits of the intellect and its emotional associations we are always left wanting! This is the most important understanding that any of us can arrive at and is the entryway to the path of freedom.

This path for me was a rocky one, that in the end I would trade for nothing. The lessons learned these past years have inspired me to chart a course that others may follow. The path is old and well-trodden with many guideposts along the route. This is the path of heart and I invite you to join me on it. All it takes to walk on this path is a willingness to surrender!

What does it Mean to Surrender?

We have all heard this term used in a religious context many times, and if you are like me you were probably confused by it. This term never sat well with me, as it sounded too much like I was giving over my free will to something outside of me. Even when I first approached it through a Buddhist perspective, I was still trying to find something to surrender to. Later I realized the truth is that there is no one to surrender to and no one to surrender. The path to that understanding is a winding one that is appropriately summed up with the saying, "You can't get there from here!" What I mean is that, as long as we choose to defend our identity through the stories we repeat each day, we remain separate from that which we truly are. So, to get to this place we must recognize that we are already there! Right this very moment! This can be viewed as a karmic pendulum swinging initially in a wide arc that pulls us between our past and future stories, with the distance gradually being reduced until it finally comes to rest at center. This demonstrates the truth that we are all already enlightened and that all we need to do is stop feeding energy into this process and allow ourselves to return to the stillness of our Primal Nature.

The Primal Tribe

This is the tribe that I invite you to discover, and surprisingly it is all around you. I refer to the process of joining with this tribe as "the practice of belonging" and the truth is that we are all already a part of it. Separation is and always has been an illusion whose facade is supported only by the sideways expression of our desire to love and be loved. When we acknowledge this, then we may begin the process of preparing our offering in the form of our old beliefs and their associated behaviors.

I am of course referring to our personal story, the one that has kept us from living the life that we desire and deserve. Our willingness to surrender this contrived version of who we are opens us to the natural flow of creation within and around us. In doing so, each of us invites our Inner Shaman to come forth and begin to guide us in this center of creation where we already are. This is just a name, that like so many others fails to capture the essence of who you are. Know that before naming, you existed, and after naming ends, you shall exist.

Your Inner Shaman

I could just as easily say your inner Zen Master, your inner consciousness or your subconscious mind. This is the part of you that has always been there for you, guiding you, directing you and keeping you from harm. This is the one who dwells at the center of creation and who constantly invites you to slow down your pendulum enough to visit and learn. She may come to you in your dreams or meditations as a beautiful woman, a sage, an old beggar or a young child. He takes any form necessary to deliver the message of who you truly are, constantly inviting you to return home. Her message is always the same, "Wake up, wake up, the world awaits your return!"

17. A Shaman's Dream

I am standing on a hillside with Ten Bears and below us is a tribe of people who live in yurts. The area beneath us is covered with these structures and people are going about their daily routines as a massive army of Roman centurion's approaches. As we look on, the soldiers go through a transformation, becoming different armies throughout the ages. Ten Bears offers, "It's always been this way!" We continue to watch this unfold as he says, "The oppressor takes myriad forms and it has always been this way."

I look on in fascination as the tribe begins to move as a unit. A single adult enters every yurt simultaneously and pulls what looks like a large round decorative shield from the top of each one. They raise the shields over their heads, firmly gripping two handles while their families hold on to them. The wind comes up and the whole tribe rises as one and is carried for some distance before they are set back down. They are safe and out of harm's way! This is the greatest lesson that any of us can learn today about the art of conflict resolution. Though the enemy appears to us in many forms, the source of our conflict remains the same, and to find it, we need only look within ourselves and let it go!

18. Tribalize Now

How do you change the world? The answer is one mind a time, start with yours! You have an opportunity with the life you have been given to celebrate the act of being human. There is a movement that is happening on a global level and no one on this planet is excluded. It is an awakening of human potential and the form it takes is up to you. It is an action of unification through dissolution of the old story.

The old story is one of separation and unworthiness, of belief in scarcity and limitation. Its core premise is that if you have enough then I will not. This is of course a fabrication that serves as the linchpin upon which the illusion of separation is hinged. Identify the old story by first becoming a good listener and choose to make a difference. Listen to your personal narrative and see it for what it is and begin to question its effect on your current circumstance. Is it helping you be more or less conscious?

Listen to others as well and hear what they are really saying about their world as they see it. Find something that you like about other people, let them know and you may find that people enjoy your company. It's okay to like people on Facebook though liking them in person is a lot more satisfying. Let me ask that question I started with. How do you change the world? You change it one heart at a time, so open yours and experience the magic of connection. Tribalize Now is all about connection on a heart level and when we choose to make it our purpose we not only change our lives, we change our world.

19. Create Your Transformative Tale

If you could transform your world what would it be like? Let your dream expand until you are able to envision the life that you desire. This is the first step on your journey of creating a life lived with intention. The next step is to take the action to unfold it, as a dream without action is only a wish. When you choose to take action you will find others willing to join with you in this quest. In order to assist you in unfolding your dream you will find an Intentional Outcome creation tool in the Offerings section of Primalcoaching.org and this is just one of many that are available to you from within the Primal Toolbox. Visit the website for information, and look for free trial membership offers to the Primal Circle where we are engaged in the process of unfolding our dreams. I am honored to present you with this invitation to join our tribe of heart; the rest is up to you.

The Primal Coaching Glossary

Please note that many new concepts and some new words are presented here and that you may need to browse further into the glossary to find an explanation of a term that is used.

Primal Coaching Invites you to harness the wisdom of the ages, to guide you through the process from dreaming it, to doing it! This is accomplished through the utilization of the Primal Toolbox, a Change Strategy based on tribal models.

Tribe Traditional tribes are communities comprised of groups of people that share both a geographic location and common interests. They also share the ethic and mores around which they form an integral unit. It is the formation of this unit that provides the template for our Primal Coaching Tribes. We refer to this template as an Intentional Core, the place from which Relational Excellence originates, and feel that this is the missing element in so much of our modern interaction. Without an Intentional Core our relationships are often no more than negotiated transactions that create a tenuous truce that requires either constant enforcement or renegotiation to be maintained.

Primal Coaching Tribes Groups of people who share principles and norms that are grounded in Relational Excellence and its practices. Shared geographic location is no longer a prerequisite for membership, though you will naturally be drawn to those with whom you share an Intentional Core.

Primal Nature Our Primal Nature is the undefiled state that is inherent in the being. Each of us is born with it, though it soon becomes obscured without an environment that nurtures and sustains it. It is this supportive environment and the Relational Excellence it fosters that we are developing through Primal Coaching.

Intention The result of one's actions whether consciously or unconsciously directed. It is unconsciously directed intention that prevents us from creating the outcomes we desire.

Unconscious Intention The results of one's action when they originate from an emotional state that is conditioned. This is a place of being at the effect of, and feeling oppressed by, our environment. Our choices and actions are supported and justified by our personal story and the results will always align with it.

Conscious Intention The application of Conscious Intention over time insures that the desired results are achieved. Using Primal Coaching tools and practices will align both our conscious and unconscious mind towards this end. Conscious Intention is a directed action that springs from a conscious awareness of our choices.

Intentional Outcomes The ability to create and sustain an Intentional Outcome that meets certain intended conditions is an essential practice of Primal Coaching. The use of the Change Modules and alignment with our Intentional Core will insure that the intended conditions are met.

Intention Cycle This is a cycle of directed intention that is sustained within the Change Modules and that serves as a feedback loop to keep us tracking our Intentional Outcome.

Intentional Core This center forms itself around the three primary attributes of Duty, Devotion and Purpose, and insures that actions originating from here align with our Intentional Outcome. Over time these primary or adolescent attributes become internalized and transformed into the adult attributes of Courage, Conviction and Strength. Our fully matured Intentional Core is in effect, including what we stand for as individuals or as a group.

Duty A moral commitment that results in action that is directed towards a cause. This is done from a view beyond limited self interest. It is activated from the concern for the greater good. Directed from a deep understanding that duty is an offering of our gift to another, to our tribe or society. Most important, it is a debt that we owe ourselves as human beings. To freely give of ourselves opens us to the rich full and abundant life that we desire and deserve.

Devotion A consistent action overtime towards a cause. This creative force contains the idea of duration both in and beyond time. It is a movement that never stops or slows. Just as one day leads to another in an unending passage of time, the goal itself is already realized unconsciously. All that is required is the conscious unfoldment of it. Effort that springs from the certainty of unconscious realization is resolute action.

Purpose That which gives meaning to our actions. It is the intentional offering of our gifts that in return actualizes them. This little understood dichotomy is the wellspring of all good in human relations. This single action creates in the being a state of joy.

Courage The ability to stand up or face danger, fear, or intimidation at risk of physical pain or threat of death. It also has a moral component that enables one to stand in their truth and defend it through speech or action. This is referred to by Ten Bears as being the "requiredness of the situation."

Conviction Standing with and acting from a certainty or belief that ensures our actions align with our truth. This is the source of resolute action.

Strength The folding and welding of pieces of high and low carbon steel in a Samurai sword or Katana combined with rapid cooling create a strong yet flexible weapon. It is this tensile strength achieved through repeatedly testing the steel that provides the metaphor for strength. It is through repeated testing that one acquires the fortitude, power, potency and expertise that are the qualities representative of true strength.

Enthusiasm This word's original meaning has evolved over time, from being infused by the breath of the divine, to today referring to it as being inspired! It is inspired joyful action or joy in action. When these actions initiate in the Intentional Core they are naturally directed towards our Intentional Outcome.

Unfoldment This is a word used to describe the ongoing creation and revelation of one's Conscious Intention. It is the offering of our talents or gifts towards an Intentional Outcome that sets this cycle in motion.

The Four Stages of Awareness This provides an effective standard for understanding where we are in our developmental process. It is effective for assessing competency in skill development, but even more profound in evaluating behavior change. In the context of the Primal Toolbox it marks our journey from a life lived unconsciously to a life lived with Conscious Intention. Each of these stages comprises tribes who share a common language and world view as people naturally gravitate to others who share their mind set. The ability to identify the stage of your tribe (employees, co-workers, family etc.) enables you to move yourself or your group forward towards a goal. Please note that these stages are but a reflection of temporary states of awareness and that all of us move back and forth between them on our journey towards the fourth stage. The four stages are as follows.

Unconscious Incompetence This is the default mode of the human being, a form of somnambulism that leaves us always at the effect of circumstance. This stage is governed by the effects of Unconscious Intention, and we find ourselves often repeating behaviors that produce unwanted outcomes without understanding the connection. The language that defines us at this level of self awareness is that of oppression and blame. We feel as if we are being crushed by external as well as internal forces and our dialogue reflects this. We are prone to isolation, though we share our misery with others when opportunity presents itself. Movement from this stage is arrived at through one of two gateways: hope or desperation. Though most of us choose desperation, either may awaken us to the next stage where we may begin to accept responsibility for our actions.

Conscious Incompetence This is the beginning of a movement towards self responsibility that is ignited by the willingness to look at the consequences of our choices. It is a difficult stage as the tendency is to retreat into unconsciousness, when faced with our unproductive behaviors that are governed by ineffective strategies. This is the stage where we begin to become aware of our old behaviors and are presented with a choice. We can challenge them and move into the third stage or feel overwhelmed by them. It is the incremental nature of change that is most difficult to grasp. The truth is that lasting change is always arrived at through consistent daily application of Conscious Intention, that when followed will lead to desirable outcomes. Constant action over time produces results and utilizing the Change Modules contained within the toolbox will assist us in tracking where we are in the process. This affords us the opportunity to make adjustments and stay on course as our life continues to unfold.

Conscious Competence This stage is where we begin to experience that sense of freedom that is born of personal responsibility. This empowering feeling comes from having put in place the limits that we have up until now resisted. These limits will vary according to the outcomes that we have selected to focus on. As an example, if it is our intention to have a long and prosperous life, then two easy areas to emphasize would be health and wellness as well as fiscal planning. How many of us arrive at retirement with either one or both of these areas lacking? Success in both of these worthy aims involves placing limitations, in one case on our expenditures, and in the other on both our choice and quantity of food that we eat, as well as perhaps limiting our hours on the couch. Though these limits are put in place in the second stage, they become a practice in the third and begin to bear fruit.

Unconscious Competence This stage is where we reap the benefits of our behavior changes and are living more productive and fulfilling lives. We operate from an Intentional Core and are now practicing with Conscious Intention while utilizing the Change Modules to insure that we are on track with our short-term goals, as well as aligning with our life's purpose. These are the unconditional attributes of Relational Excellence that produce Conscious Stage Four Tribes.

Conscious Stage Four Tribes These are defined by Relational Excellence. This is the focus of all interactions and this single principle that emanates from its Intentional Core has the potential to change how we create our future as a species on this planet.

Individual Excellence This is far from the limiting concept of perfection! It is our best effort each day directed towards an Intentional Outcome. This shifts our perspective from an externally driven measure to one of acknowledging the value of our efforts from within ourselves. Using the Change Modules each day gives us the ability to honestly assess our efforts and make adjustments.

Enterprise Excellence When organizations or businesses choose Enterprise Excellence, defined here as an operational model that embraces Relational Excellence, the results will be far reaching. It starts with the employees and spreads throughout your customer base to the community. Strategies that are grounded in Relational Excellence are directed towards an Intentional Outcome that encompasses the long-term consequences of our actions when calculating short-term profitability.

Relational Excellence The principles and norms which thriving individuals and enterprises exhibit when operating from an Intentional Core that is aligned with a group's Operational Core. When you practice Relational Excellence your actions spring from consideration for the outcomes that they produce. Whether individual or enterprise in origin we always ask the question, "How does that affect?" when contemplating our options and strategies. The formulation and implementation of these when based on an Intentional Outcome will yield the desired results.

Change Strategy A comprehensive application of tools and processes directed towards a goal.

Primal Toolbox The Primal (Original) Toolbox is a Change Strategy based on methods utilized by tribal people to empower individuals to become conscious valued members of their family, tribe or community.

Change Modules The four modules comprise one full cycle of directed creative action. This Intention Cycle is based on four transitional stages that provide the template upon which our intention may be nurtured, cultivated and received.

Creation Module This is where the creative process takes shape! It begins with an idea that is allowed to expand. We then pull our vision back in, until it fits all of the parameters of an Intentional Outcome. We must now check its alignment with our Intentional Core and explore its probable future to insure its unimpeded unfoldment. The seeds of success are sown and begin to take root.

Development Module This module fosters applied action over time that is directed towards an Intentional Outcome. This requires the full utilization and consistent application of one's resources undeviating from the Intentional Core. This is done with the knowledge that the desired result is awaiting us and that all that is required is consistent action day in and day out in the form of Individual Excellence.

Fulfillment Module This is the place of receiving that which flows from our consistent action over time. The desired result is apparent as we are now bearing witness to the fruits of our labor. This is the time of harvest, of making full use of this period of abundance. It is also a time of celebration, of acknowledging all the effort that was directed towards this end. This festivity is a communal ceremony that gives thanks to Individual Excellence as a natural expression of Relational Excellence.

Completion Module The final stage is one of reflection and contemplation, of reviewing the effects of our actions and asking, "Is what we have accomplished completely aligned with our Core Intention?" This practice is used at the end of projects or tasks to insure that all of the value of the experience has been gleaned and nothing left undone. This final stage is one that is often neglected in our high-paced modern life. This is the element that when used daily will assure that our actions are both sufficient and directed towards our Intentional Outcome. Checking congruence as a practice keeps us tracking our Conscious rather than Unconscious Intention. The seasons of the year and their transition points provide tribal people with a template that marks their progress. This practice endured in more complex cultures such as ancient China where it was customary to close the gates of the empire during the winter solstice for a ten-day period of reflection and contemplation. People were encouraged to discard unproductive practices and begin the new year with a clean slate and renewed intention.

Transformational Tales These are stories of becoming that represent the realization of the Intentional Outcome that we put in place. We are defined by the stories we tell ourselves, families, friends and co-workers each day. The repetition of these stories is either a catalyst for change or an excuse to remain securely in the status quo. Our tribe is composed of those who share our story! We easily form associations with them based on our current worldview, as well as the stories we express both verbally and non-verbally that support it. In the context of the Primal Toolbox, this consists of a series of guided visualizations and stories that are designed to awaken our awareness on a conscious as well as subconscious level. These are contained within the four modules and are used to assist us on our journey around the wheel.

Coyote Medicine In the tradition of Native American spirituality that I was taught, the coyote or raven are seen as messengers that deliver communication from the subconscious to the conscious mind in ways that bypass the critical factor (ego). These messages may conflict with the personal story that has supported our current behaviors or beliefs and will present us with an opportunity to have a "look see" as Ten Bears called it. These could be non-productive behaviors or they could be gifts or talents that we are not yet ready to own. This medicine may be administered by a skillful practitioner such as my mentor, though more often they will originate as synchronous occurrences throughout our day that are urging us to pay attention.

Sacred Medicine The teachings and practices that tribal people venerate, the elements that are passed from generation to generation assuring the continuity of its Intentional Core. Though the healing practices that consisted of herbal medicines and prayers are a part of this, the reference here is to the Operational Core that supports the Intentional Core.

Operational Core These are the teachings and practices that in tribal cultures arise from the Intentional Core and that define what the tribe stands for as a people. These are in effect the Sacred Medicine that hold the tribe intact from generation to generation through the transmission of its core values. A simplistic view would be that the Operational Core is to the Intentional Core as an Operations Manual is to the Mission Statement of a corporation, whether it be financial, non-profit, union, political or any organization formed around a cause. This comparison is actually more appropriate than first surmised! What we hold sacred defines who we are as a people. It defines what we stand for, and what we will defend with everything in our power. Tribal people defend what is sacred to them even to their death, and corporations could be said to be doing the same. The question I would pose is, what is it that corporations hold sacred? Is it the wellbeing of its members from the CEO to all of the various workers? Is it the community that they operate in and how they affect it? Is it their shareholders? Is it those that they trade with and how those trades are conducted? What is it that forms the Intentional Core of our corporate citizens or even our political structure that is composed of two main tribes, with an ever-growing third one of independents? These questions, when asked, empower us to choose whom we do business with, or vote for, as we are the enablers of our corporations' behaviors as well as that of our elected officials. In either case we have an ability to express our disapproval and hold them accountable when their words and actions are incongruous. How different might our world be, if these entities were encouraged to evolve along with us into Conscious Stage Four Tribes?

Resources

Adyashanti. *The End of Your World.* Sounds True Inc. 2008, 2010

Peter Block. *Community. The Structure of Belonging.* Berrett-Koehler Publishers, Inc. 2008

Black Elk, Wallace and William S. Lyon. *Black Elk: The Sacred Ways of a Lakota.* HarperCollins Publisher. New York, New York. 1991

Brown, Joseph Epes. *The Sacred Pipe: Black Elk's Account of the Seven Rites of the Oglala Sioux.* MJF Books New York, New York. 1953, 1989

Dyer, DR. Wayne. *Excuses Begone! How to Change Lifelong, Self-Defeating Thinking Habits.* Hay House Inc. 2009

Diamond, Jared. *Guns, Germs and Steel: The Fates of Human Societies.* W.W. Norton, 1997

Diamond, Jared. *The World Until Yesterday: What can we Learn from Traditional Societies?* The Penguin Group, 2012

Duhigg, Charles. *The Power of Habit: Why We Do What We Do In Life And Business.* Random House Inc. 2012

Gilligan, Stephen. *Generative Trance: The Experience of Creative Flow.* Crown House Publishing U.K. 2012

Godin, Seth. *Linchpin: Are You Indispensable?* Penguin Group, New York, New York, 2010

Godin, Seth. *Tribes: We Need You to Lead Us.* Portfolio a member of The Penguin Group, 2008

Hoffman, Michael. *Your Natural Gift: Offering the Essence of Your Heart.* Stillpoint Books, 2013

Dave Logan, John King & Halee Fischer-Wright. *Tribal Leadership: Leveraging Natural Groups to Build a Thriving Organization.* HarperCollins Publishers, 2008

Mlodinow, Leonard. *Subliminal: How your Unconscious Mind Rules Your Behavior.* Random House, Inc. 2012

Ross, Carne. *The Leaderless Revolution: How Ordinary People Will Take Power and Change Politics in the 21st Century.* blue rider press, The Penguin Group,. New York, New York, 2011

Smith, Charles Hugh. *Survival+: Structuring Prosperity for Yourself and the Nation.* Oftwominds.com, Berkeley, California 2010

Smith, Charles Hugh. *The Nearly Free University & The Emerging Economy.* Oftwominds.com, Berkeley, California 2013

Tolle, Eckhart. *The Power of Now: A Guide To Spiritual Enlightenment.* New World Library, Navato, California 1997

www.ingramcontent.com/pod-product-compliance
Lightning Source LLC
Chambersburg PA
CBHW052114090426
42741CB00009B/1808